Acknowledgments

I would like to thank everyone that has helped make this book possible including my wife Candace who helped with the editing and helped keep our three boys quiet as I wrote and assembled this undertaking.

I would also like to thank my parents whom I love very dearly. Even today I continue to miss my biological mother and I am thankful to God for putting my second mother, Connie, into my life.

Deep thanks go out to my brother who contributed much needed advice, to Ben Brotbeck and his wife Mechele, and to Lee and Bette for all of their help.

I would like to thank everyone who so graciously allowed me to share their defining moments with the hope of inspiring others to follow their dreams and to learn from the lessons that life has to offer.

I'd like to thank Willard Filley, Charles Yue, Dean Cota, Bucky Burgau, Craig Richie, Judy Siegle, Thomas Jefferson, Caline Olson, Jim Holthus, Tim Bauer, Bethany Heen, Minh Tran, Deb Jevne, Ernie Mancini, Ginny Kruger and Glen, Julie and Carol Brookshire.

A special thanks goes out to Anita Dittman who allowed me to reprint a chapter from her book. I would strongly encourage anyone interested in purchasing her book to contact me to make arrangements. It's well worth the read.

Introduction

Throughout the years I have had numerous youth ask me why I am the way I am.

"Why do you coach...preach...teach...tell corny jokes... write for the newspaper?" These are just a few of the questions teenagers have asked me as they are struggling with the issues of growing up.

As I thought about these questions I often came to several events in my life that defined who I was from that point on. As I discussed this concept with others I found out that everyone seemed to be able to immediately identify their own defining moments.

Often times these defining moments are spiritual events in one's life while some are times of great revelation. Another thing I found was that many people don't realize how defining the moment is until they are able to reflect on the event in the days, months and years that follow.

I would hope that this book is inspirational, motivational and worth your time to read it. If you would like to share your own defining moments with me I would encourage you to write to me and tell me what it is. You never know it could end up in a second book. There has already been talk about <u>Life's Defining Moments 2</u>.

        Chad A. Filley
        Box 193
        Halstad, MN 56548
           or
        (218) 456-2516
           or
        chadfilley@rrv.net

If you would like to order additional copies of the book you can contact me at either of the above addresses. Purchase price is $9.95 per copy plus $2 shipping & handling.

Also feel free to contact me if you would like a **supplemental discussion guide** for use with the book. This can be sent to you through e-mail or through U.S. Postage for a $1 charge to cover postage and handling. This guide will allow groups the opportunity to further investigate the issues involved in each story.

Thanks again and may God bless you in whatever path you take with your life.

Chad A. Filley

For Candy, Trent, Tyrel, Isaiah and all of the people that have inspired me over the years.

Filley Communications (Cross-Stitch Publishing)
405 3rd Ave. W.
Halstad, MN 56548

© 2000 by Chad A. Filley
All rights reserved. This book, or parts thereof, may not be reproduced in any form without permission.

ISBN 0-9702986-0-9 (Paperback)
LCCN 00-191505

Book Cover Design: Candy Filley and Bette Blixt.

Life's Defining Moments

Written & Compiled By:

Chad A. Filley

Hospice of the Red River Valley
1701 38th St. SW
Fargo, ND 58103

Cross-Stitch Publishing
Halstad, MN

Contents

The Cross-Stitch Picture	Chad A. Filley	1
What's In a Name	Willard Filley	9
The Birthday Party	Ginny Kruger	17
Hospitalized	Anita Dittman	19
Anniversary	Chad A. Filley	29
The Outsider	Chad A. Filley	39
Whatever it Takes	Glen & Julie Brookshire	45
The Decision	Glen Brookshire	53
Two Steps Short	Judy Siegle	57
You Don't Know What You Have Until You Almost Lose It	Chad A. Filley	67
Hiroshima	Ernie Mancini	73
The Hug Quota	Jim Holthus	83
The Crash	Deb Jevne	89

Contents

The Complete Turnaround	Bethany & Helen Heen	99
The Break	Craig Richie	107
The Bottom of the Ninth	Bucky Burgau	111
The Decision That Weighed on My Mind	Dean Cota	117
The World is a Little Less Beautiful Today	Chad A. Filley	129
For the Love of Freedom	Minh Tran	137
The Polar Bear	Anonymous	145
The Lesson	Caline Olson	151
Faith Shaping Experience	Tim Bauer	155
Don't Ever Judge a Book By its Cover	Chad A. Filley	161
Heartsick	Caline Olson	167
Career Change	Charles Yue	181
Hometown Reminiscence	Thomas Jefferson	187

The Cross-Stitch Picture
By
Chad A. Filley

    Up until the time I was eight years old I was an only child. I can still remember Mom calling me into her bedroom to tell me she was going to have a baby. Mom must have anticipated things getting a little rough for me; after all I had been the only kid on the block. For the next few months she went out of her way to spend some quality time with me before the arrival of the newborn.
    Evening after evening I would cuddle next to her on the couch as she sang the song "You are my Sunshine, my only Sunshine..." This song always left me with a sad feeling because it ends with the line "Please don't take my Sunshine away." As a young child I always thought how sad it would be to have your Sunshine taken away.
    As we cuddled she was making this cross-stitch picture with a little brown-haired boy sitting next to his dog. It just happened to look like a puppy we had once owned. The statement on the bottom of the cross-stitch photo is a poem that describes little boys. It always reminded me of the poem that says that little boys are made of snips and snails and puppy dog tails. I always found that to be a rip-off considering that little girls got to be made of sugar and spice and everything nice, but nonetheless the cross-stitch

picture meant a great deal to me. It was Mom's last gift to me before the arrival of the new baby.

The months passed and before I knew it Mom went in to the hospital and had a healthy baby boy, but there were complications and she died.

She never came home. My Sunshine had been taken away.

Being eight-years-old nobody bothered to sit down and explain just what had happened to me. As you can imagine everyone was in total shock when a relatively healthy young woman went into the hospital and didn't come home. Everyone was having enough trouble coping with their own acceptance of this tragedy, so trying to explain what had happened to a young child was probably next to impossible for most.

The third-hand information that filtered down to me basically said that the nurse in charge of the emergency room, the one that was supposed to be watching her as she recovered, had slipped out of the room to have a cigarette while my mother had vomited and aspirated. I had been told that when the nurse came back she was dead. As anyone could imagine I grew up with a great deal of anger. Someone had killed my mother.

Other than that I always felt I had a normal childhood. I laughed like other kids, cried like other kids, had fun like other kids, played sports like other kids and did all kinds of things, but deep down I had anger over the loss of my mother. I blamed this person, this monster, this murderer that had stepped out for a cigarette break.

Years later my wife Candy, who was then my fiancée, and I decided that it was time to deal with this anger. We obtained my father's written permission to look through my mother's medical records from the hospital where she had died.

Candy and I walked into the hospital administrator's office, handed her the permission slips and waited as she retrieved the files for us. She then proceeded to photocopy all of the records for us.

"Is there any chance I could speak to the doctor?"

She explained that he had recently retired and moved to Florida.

"Boy that sure is convenient," I thought to myself.

I then looked at the records and saw the name of the nurse anesthetist on the bottom of one of the pages, so I asked about her.

"She's retired too, but she and her husband (she gave his name) still live in town," she said.

"You don't happen to know her address do you?" I asked.

"Just a minute and I'll check for you," she said heading into the lobby to get the information.

As we sat waiting I heard the other administrator ask her what she was doing. She briefly explained the situation and then I heard something that sounded very odd to me at the time.

"You can't give him that," he said "He could go over to her house and kill her."

I had never thought of that, but I did hate the very beast that was responsible for my mother's death.

The administrator came back into the office and apologized as she explained that it was against hospital policy to give out the address of former employees.

"That's okay," I said.

I then walked out of her office and headed straight for the nearest pay phone to look up her address in the phone book. Candy and I then proceeded to find her.

It was a hot summer day and I could instantly tell someone was home as I pulled my car in front of her house because all of her windows were open and only the screen door on her porch was closed.

As I approached the house I could hear the extremely loud television set halfway down the sidewalk. I took a deep breath and knocked on the door not knowing what to expect.

"May I help you?" the elderly lady that answered the door asked.

"My mother was a patient of yours and I was wondering if I could talk to you for a few minutes. Can I come in?"

She invited me in and I handed her the medical records. I then rudely told her to turn the volume on the television set down so we could talk. Can you imagine walking into a person's house and telling them to do this?

The anger in me began boiling up as she opened the files; after all she was my mother's murderer. I watched her open the envelope and began to page through the records. I then noticed something I hadn't counted on seeing. A tear began rolling down her cheek.

"You remember this?" I asked still engulfed by anger.

"Of course I remember. In the twenty plus years I worked as a nurse anesthetist we only lost one mother in the maternity ward and that was your mom". "What happened?" I said wanting the long overdue explanation.

She looked through the charts and told me that they did everything they could. She had started to bleed internally and her condition worsened throughout the night. Not expecting to have any type of surgery she had eaten the day before giving birth and the anesthesia caused her to vomit. The vomit backed up into her lungs and the hospital staff attempted to vacuum them out, but it was of no use.

As the woman spoke with me I could tell that she was sincere. There's no way she could have looked me in the eyes and faked tears if she didn't genuinely care.

"I don't know if this will make you feel any better, but these very eyes that are crying were the last one's that your mother ever looked into," she said. She explained that people going under are often terrified and it was always rewarding for her to know that she could be a comfort to them during these trying times.

Her tears were much like a baptism to me. All of these years of anger and hatred of the monster that had killed my mother were gone. It was an uplifting experience for me to confront my demon and find out that she really wasn't the evil creature that I believed she was.

A couple months later my stepmother, Connie, called. Dad and she thought it would be a good idea for my brother and I to divide up some of my mother's heirlooms before my wedding. I always thought this was kind of weird. A person's entire life ends up being a few heirlooms that get divided up among family members.

We agreed to meet on a certain date and just before I was about to hang up Connie said, "Oh, by the way, you can have anything, but your brother would like to keep that old cross-stitch picture that hangs in his bedroom."

It was just about like I was hit in the stomach with a sledgehammer. How could anyone want this cross-stitch photo? It was mine. Mom had made it for me.

I honestly believe that if I hadn't confronted the nurse there would have been no way I would have been able to give it up. That experience had changed my life.

Candy and I talked things over and we decided that if it meant that much to my brother then he should have it. After all I was the lucky one. I was fortunate enough to have had eight wonderful years with my Sunshine and he only had one day. I had many great memories and he had none. If that wall hanging meant that much to him than he should have it.

It was always neat when I would come back and visit him and see a teenager's wall plastered with posters, tae kwon do belts and a cross-stitch picture with a little brown-haired boy and his puppy.

Whenever I saw it I knew that mom was there with him.

If you would like to contact Chad Filley for a speaking engagement, additional copies of the book or to let him know a defining moment of your own you can reach him at:

Chad A. Filley
Box 193
Halstad, MN 56548
  or
(218) 456-2516
  or
chadfilley@rrv.net

What's in a Name?

(An experience in the life of Willard Filley as told to his grandson Chad)

"There weren't very many happy days in my childhood," Willard said referring to his days in rural Montana during the great depression. "Mom died when I was ten years old and Pa was too busy getting drunk to care for me and my brothers and sisters."

Willard's mother had been as caring a person as you could find, but she had made one poor choice when she married Eugene. He was neglectful and a chronic drinker, so leaving the children in his care was out of the question.

It was decided that Willard's brother Lawrence (age 7), his sister's Florence (age 13) and Bonnie (age 3) along with Willard would have to go live with their Grandma Maude in Nebraska.

"Somehow my good-for-nothing father finagled Grandma into buying him a ticket to come with to Nebraska," Willard told. It wasn't an easy sale for Eugene to talk his mother-in-law into bringing him back because she never approved of him or his drinking, and she wasn't afraid to let him know.

"Grandma paid for the tickets in Nebraska," Willard explained, "And she made sure that it was impossible to cash them in. She was probably afraid he would cash them in for some whiskey."

Life wasn't easy on Grandma Maude's farm

and it certainly wasn't going to get any easier with four young children living there. Grandpa had died in 1927 and Grandma had lost all of her money when the town bank closed. Managing to stay afloat on her 80-acre farm was close to impossible, but she gave it her best effort.

Her house had no electricity; little food and her meager source of income came from doing laundry for a local Jewish family that owned the store in town.

"Grandma used to bribe us kids with a teaspoon of brown sugar to get us to pump the washing machine all day," he explained.

Things eventually got to the point where it was just too much for one little old lady to take care of these four children. She was receiving no help from Eugene who usually sat in town at the bar. Maude finally ended up going to the county and asking for some relief, but there weren't any funds available.

After asking a second time the county held a court hearing and it was decided that three of the children should be placed into the Christian Home for Children in Council Bluffs, Iowa. Florence was now old enough to be able to work at a local family's house in exchange for room and board, but the rest of the kids were headed for the home.

"Dad brought us kids to the office. He went into the office while us kids waited in the hallway," Willard explained. "He didn't even say good-bye to us. He just walked on down the hall." (Willard began to cry).

Bonnie screamed "Dad don't leave us here!"

He didn't pay any attention. He just kept on walking.

"Imagine how you feel when your own dad abandons you," Willard said.

The Christian Home ran primarily on donations and did a good job caring for the 100 plus kids that it housed. Most of the kids living there came from broken families.

"The sad part was on the weekends," Willard said. "On Sunday afternoon lots of company would come to visit the other kids, but we never had anybody come."

Grandma wrote occasionally and every so often Willard's older brothers would send any extra cash they could scrape together, but he never once heard from his dad.

"The Christian Home wasn't that bad," he explained. "But it wasn't ever home. On Saturdays they would march all of the children down to see a picture show in town and I even got to see Blackstone the Magician.

"It wasn't too long before Bonnie was adopted out to a local family," Willard said. "I got to go with her to see the family, but then I had to go back to the Home after she had settled in." They adopted her and she became part of her new family.

"I guess I was just too old to adopt," he said.

It wasn't too long after that when Lawrence disappeared from the home. Nobody even bothered to tell Willard where he had gone.

"All they would tell me was that he was still alive," he said.

Willard later found out that his brother had gone to live with a family in Northern Iowa. One Sunday that family went to spend an afternoon at the local park where they happened to run into his Great Uncle Roy and Aunt Mamie. Roy spotted Lawrence and talked the family into allowing them to take him home with them to care for him.

"It would have been nice if they had sent for me too," Willard said.

"After losing both my brother and my sister another kid talked me into running away with him to go live with his dad," he said.

The twosome hid when the supper bell rang and took off for the Missouri Valley to see his dad. It soon got dark.

"We hid whenever a car would stop," he explained. "Eventually the kids dad ended up finding us. He didn't even yell at us. He just brought us back to the Home."

Willard was pleasantly surprised, as he didn't receive the harsh punishment he expected upon going back to the Home.

"All the head lady did was give us a lecture," he said. "She told us she'd replace us with people that wanted to be there and then she sent us to class."

Willard was now thirteen years old. One day Willard was called into the office. There was a farming couple that was looking for a boy.

"I was excited at first. Finally somebody wanted to adopt me," Willard said. "But I soon found out they were just looking for a cheap hired man. Nothing more than a slave."

The first thing the man did was comment on Willard's size and point out that he would be strong enough to help with the chores. The family agreed to pay him a dollar a month and he would be in charge of buying his own clothing, schoolbooks and saving his own spending money.

"I ended up doing all of the work," he said. "The man was extremely lazy. I had to milk all 25 cows before I could go to school." Most mornings Willard didn't even get to school before 10 a.m. The teacher, Ms. Swisher, understood the problem and never once marked Willard tardy.

Whenever the Smith's would go to town, which was often two or more times a week, Willard was responsible for milking all of the cows and feeding the hogs.

"During the first year out of the 52 dollars I was supposed to have gotten I still had $40 coming," Willard said. "He told me they couldn't afford to pay me."

Instead of paying Willard they gave him a pig to have in 4-H.

"This was during the time when people were killing livestock because they weren't worth the feed you put into them," Willard said. "I ended up selling the hog for $9.40. Not much return on a whole year's work."

Willard took the money and bought new clothes and shoes for school in the fall. After he had bought the clothing the Smith's told him they weren't going to send him to high school. They wanted him to stay on the farm full-time.

    Jim Roberts, a neighbor down the road, often mentioned to Willard that if things got too rough that he could always live with him. One morning Mr. Smith's three-year-old son shut the door on the double corncrib killing a couple of the chickens. Mr. Smith got a belt and tied the dead chicken to the boy and made him drag it around the rest of the day.

    "To this day I can't forget the way the boy screamed," Willard said. Feeling bad for the boy he attempted to take the belt off the boy, but Mr. Smith screamed at him. The two of them got into an argument and Willard left for the Roberts' farm. He ended up living with the Roberts' family for a week. During that week Archie Kirlin, the rural mail carrier came to talk to him.

    He explained that he had seen how cruel Mr. Smith had been and felt like he could help out. Kirlin had two daughters and really wanted a son. He asked Willard to come and live with his family. Willard went to live with Archie and his wife.

    Archie went to his good friend the sheriff to see if there was anything he could do. The sheriff felt that at the very least he could go out to Smith's farm to get his clothes back, but they had already sold them. The sheriff threatened to arrest Smith for what he had done, but Smith reminded the sheriff that he was related to one of the county commissioners. The sheriff decided to take Willard and back off. Archie then took Willard to town and bought him some brand new clothes.

"Archie and his wife Pearl were very good to me. They included me in everything. I was finally part of a family once again. It had been a long time," he explained. "It felt good."

Willard lived with the Kirlin's for the next couple of years and felt what it was like to be a part of a loving, caring family.

"I always told Archie that if I ever had a son I would name him after him," Willard said. "He told me that if I did that he would buy the boy a new suit."

Willard eventually left the Kirlin's to make his own mark on the world and truly regretted never getting the chance to have one last chance to tell Archie how much he appreciated him before he died.

"He was a much better father than my real one had ever been."

Willard was daily reminded of his surrogate father whenever he called out his first son's name.

"On May 19, 1939, your father, my oldest son, was born and I kept my promise and named him Archie. Kirlin also lived up to his end of the bargain and bought him a brand new suit."

(It's kind of funny when you find out your dad really was named after the mailman.)

When Archie and Pearl died Willard was given one-third of their estate, but that was nothing compared to the love they had given him years before.

The Birthday Party
By
Ginny Kruger

When Muria, our third grade daughter, popped off the school bus, I knew something was up. Excitedly she yelled to me from the end of the driveway, "It's gonna be Jeanna's birthday, and she's gonna have a party."

Later that evening, she asked if there was any extra work around the house that needed to be done.

"I've been thinking," she said, "I want to give Jeanna a real nice present and it's no good if you give me money to buy a gift. I want to earn money to buy it... You know she is my very bestest special friend."

A deal was struck, the money was earned and a trip to the shopping mall was made. The shopping trip was memorable because of the intensity and duration; what was purchased is long forgotten.

Arriving home, her blue eyes glistening, Muria stated, "I've been thinking, it's no good if you use that 'boughten' wrapping paper. I'm gonna make my own. Jeanna is my very bestest special friend and I want this present to be as special as she is."

Out came the tempera paints, the freezer paper and a potato to carve. She made potato print wrapping paper.

With the paint dried and the gift wrapped Muria asked if she could have a sheet of my best writing paper.

"I've been thinking," she said, "I want to make a birthday card for Jeanna, cause you can never buy one that says just what you want to say and she is my very bestest special friend."

After several hours of diligent work, the card was firmly affixed to the present with plenty of tape. The present was then placed on the dining room table to await the birthday party.

The present waited...and waited...and waited.

Muria never was asked to the birthday party.

"And it was a slumber party Mom," she said. "I've never been to a slumber party."

When the tears were finished and a question was asked about what to do with the future gift, Muria slowly responded, "I've been thinking about that. I'm gonna give Jeanna the gift anyway; you know, she is my very bestest special friend..."

Children often have wisdom beyond their years, and share it with us when we are willing to listen. Their sense of friendship can run deep, at any age.

Ginny Kruger is a story-telling inspirational speaker living in Northwestern Minnesota. If you are interested in contacting her concerning a potential speaking engagement she can be reached through e-mail at gkrugerspeaks@hotmail.com

Hospitalized

(An excerpt from the book "Trapped in Hitler's Hell" from the life of Anita Dittman as told to Jan Markell)

Anita is a Jewish Christian that suffered in a Nazi work camp during World War II. She escaped from the camp just prior to the excerpt you are about to read.

Bautzen was a clean little town that had escaped the war's destruction. Ushci's relatives pampered us when we found them, and they took me to the hospital almost immediately. I could see that the hospital was run by the Nazis, and something about them told me they still hadn't given up the "glorious" dream of the Third Reich.

The head nurse, Miss Grete, had cut away my sock, which clung to my swollen leg. The infection had driven my temperature to nearly 105 degrees.

While she worked on my leg Miss Grete looked at me, the ugly Nazi pin on her uniform transfixing my gaze. Obviously she didn't appreciate the fact that I didn't respond to her "Heil Hitler" when we met. She gave me a skimpy hospital gown and walked me to a room at the end of the hall. I climbed between the clean, white sheets, almost delirious from fever. However, it seemed that I was placed at the bottom of the staff's priority list; I lay for hours waiting for treatment. Finally I lost track of all time as I drifted in and out of consciousness. Often I heard footsteps in the hall, but they never came to my room.

Two days later emergency surgery was performed: two holes were drilled into my foot to enable the infection to drain. Since ether was at a high premium, I wasn't given enough and I awakened in the middle of the surgery. Amid the pain I heard Miss Grete say, "She sure talked, didn't she, Doctor?"

I was numb with fear, sensing that I'd given myself away. My fear was confirmed the following days and weeks as the Nazi hospital neglected me in various subtle ways. Besides being left unattended for hours, I was never given any pain pills. Because I always refused to respond to Miss Grete's "Heil Hitler," she withheld the necessary sanitary bandages for my leg wound. She also rerouted the doctor's visits so that I would often miss a day or two. Due to that kind of treatment and because I developed an allergy to the medication, I had to endure six long weeks of loneliness and neglect in the hospital. Only frequent visits from (my friend) Hella made it bearable.

My leg was cut and sewed hastily and improperly in four operations. Six ugly red scars would be the result. Just prior to the last operation, a Nazi doctor said, "Anita, we must insert some more drainage tubes in your leg. This is serious because we will be working close to your artery. If it gets complicated, we may have to amputate your leg."

How I needed Mother's comforting words of assurance during those hours before my operation! What was to stop these Nazis from cutting off my leg because of their dislike for me? I could only talk to my Heavenly Father, as once again I relied totally on Him. He faithfully demonstrated His love for me, for I learned it was Miss Grete's day off that week was the day of my surgery. At least she wouldn't be in the operating room encouraging an amputation.

Again I was given only enough ether to put me into a light sleep, so I heard the voices of the doctors and nurses throughout most of the surgery. The pain was so intense that I hoped I would just black out. As I lay there gritting my teeth, I felt beneath the cover for my leg. Praise God, it was still there! I believed God would surely spare it because He knew I had a long journey to Theresienstadt (to see my mother).

I felt again as I wheeled back to my dingy room. Tears trickled out of the corners of my eyes as I realized that God's mercy had kept me in one piece.

Hella visited me that night and, as usual, kept me up to date on the war.

"The Allied troops are nearly in every major city now, Anita, and they're on the outskirts of Berlin. The war will be finished in a few days, but the bad news is that the Russians are advancing to Bautzen too. They may be here any day."

Hospice of the Red River Valley
1701 38th St. SW
Fargo, ND 58103

We had hoped and prayed that the war would end without an invasion of Bautzen, for we continued to be afraid of the Russian, not knowing how they would treat us. Would they pillage, burn, and rape, or would they liberate and restore? We had been fed horrible propaganda about the Reds. According to Hitler, they were as despicable as the Jews. How would the Russians know that Hella, Uschi and I were victims of the war and not perpetrators? These questions jumbled my thoughts as I lay recuperating.

Hella also told me that President Roosevelt had died that week. I felt so bad that the man who had stopped in and speeded up my freedom hadn't lived to see our victory celebration.

When I pulled back the covers to show Hella my ugly leg wounds, which would leave lifelong scars, she gasped.

"Don't worry, Hella," I said calmly. "Those wounds and scars will be my salvation. God has impressed that on me as I've been lying here all of these weeks. He says all things work together for our good, and so will these wounds."

That week Hella came to the hospital and helped me learn to walk again. I worked frantically to get back the strength in my leg so that I could make the long journey into Czechoslovakia to find Mother.

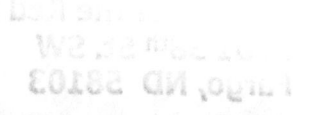

More than six weeks after I'd been admitted to the hospital I was told I could leave. That morning I awakened with renewed enthusiasm for life; my ordeal was over. But before I could even begin to collect myself or my things, I heard Miss Grete's frantic voice in the hall.

"Out of bed, all who are able!" she screamed. "Get dressed immediately and go to the air-raid shelter. The Russians are in Bautzen! Hurry up!"

I struggled to get dressed as the frightened hospital staff and patients scurried about, but I was still weak and had very little strength in my one leg. Even so, that unexplainable peace from God came over me again.

As I reached for the cane I'd been given, I heard gunfire in the streets. Intermittently I also heard the sound of cannon fire; we all knew that one blast from a Russian cannon would level a building.

Slowly I moved down the hall, leaning on the wall and balancing on my cane. When Miss Grete saw me with the cane, she yanked it from me; I nearly crashed to the floor.

"That old lady over there needs this!" she insisted. "Go and help her into the shelter."

"Oh dear God, give me the double strength," I pleaded softly. Only God could strengthen and steady me as I balanced both the elderly patient and myself going down the shelter stairs.

Nearly a hundred patients and staff walked, ran or were pushed in wheelchairs to the air-raid shelter deep beneath the hospital. Again I heard the pitiful cries of desperate people whose ailing bodies protested the move to the cold, damp shelter.

God had pity on us, for just as the air-raid shelter door closed we heard a blast of mortar tear through the hospital's first floor. We thought that surely it was an accident, that the Russians wouldn't knowingly shell a hospital caring for civilians. But then another round of mortar hit the hospital. All day long gunfire sounded in the streets as German soldiers tried to save the city, but there was no stopping the allies anymore.

I was so afraid for Hella and Uschi and her relatives. But I could only leave them in God's hands, as it seemed I had to do so often with loved ones.

For eight days we huddled in the candlelit shelter while the Germans tried in vain to save the town. Four of us patients shared one tiny bed. We could hardly move; otherwise, we would push someone to the floor. Some patients cursed while others wept or pleaded for help, but the hospital staff had been able to carry in only a few medical supplies. We had little food, and it seemed that the shelter was pitifully prepared for a long ordeal. Evidently no one had wanted to admit that a day might come when so many would be crammed into the shelter.

I tried to comfort the three elderly women who shared my bed.

"Do you know Jesus?" I asked them one by one. "Because He has promised us eternal life after death, we needn't be so afraid. He says that even if we walk through the valley of the shadow of death, we need fear nothing, for He is with us."

They listened as I comforted them and quoted a few Bible passages I had memorized. I had lost my Bible in the confusion of our prison escape. I reached into my pocket to feel my only possessions: a toothbrush, a small bar of soap, a broken comb, and the last of the money Mother had given me.

"Hitler became my god," one of the women admitted. "We thought he was such a savior of the country. He promised us so much..."

"It was only the last few months that I realized he was a demagogue," another confessed. "Such a dream, such a nightmare. Can God ever forgive us?"

"Yes He can!" I replied enthusiastically. "That is what He specializes in. He could forgive even Hitler if he asked for forgiveness. That's how gracious God is."

"I believed in God once," an old lady said, "but it is difficult to believe in him now. I've seen the ugliness. I lived in Berlin but fled to Bautzen to be with my daughter. Berlin is just a shell, you know. Most of my friends died."

"And what about your daughter?" I asked. "Is she all right?"

"How can I know when I'm trapped down here? I hear the cannon fire and gunfire outside. How do I know it isn't meant for my daughter and her family?"

"The gunfire has to be for the German soldiers and not for innocent civilians," I said, trying to comfort the old lady. "I am going to pray for your daughter now. Would you like to pray with me?"

"Yes, I would," she said.

About the fourth day of battle, it grew very quiet outside. Obviously the battle had gone one way or another and we soon received our answer as a dozen or more Russian soldiers stormed into the air-raid shelter. Everyone stood or sat frozen with fear as the Russians surveyed our pitiful lot. Carrying huge rifles with bayonets on them, they talked among themselves and began to eye the women staff and patients. Then, one by one, they grabbed some of the women and threw them to the floor. While the rest of us looked on in horror, they raped a dozen or more women.

Two of the huge soldiers came right for me. "Oh God, help me," I pleaded out loud. Pulling me from the bed, they threw me to the floor and started to rip my clothes off. It was a scene right out of hell, as man's depraved nature was personified before my eyes.

The two soldiers gazed at my unbandaged leg, with its horrible red wounds that were only partially healed. They grimaced as they saw the leg and muttered to each other. Then they shook their heads and walked away in search of a more appealing victim. So this was the salvation promised by my wounds!

When the horror ended an hour later, we all sat in a state of semi-shock, wondering what to do and where to go. Found, conquered, abandoned. Was that that? Despair wore many faces that day: fear, confusion, agony, loneliness.

Were all Germans suffering like this as they came under the guns of the allies?

I saw a woman weeping as she sat in the corner. In the darkness of the shelter I couldn't make out who it was. I limped over to see if I could help, or at least listen to her problem. It was Miss Grete. I prayed that God might give me the humility and compassion to reach out and comfort her.

I timidly knelt beside her and put my arm around her shoulder. She didn't pull away, even though she knew who I was. Instead, she leaned against my shoulder and wept. In broken sentences she told me she had been raped four times by the Russian soldiers.

"God have mercy on them," I said.

She looked up at me with her red, swollen eyes.

"How can you comfort me?" she asked. "I really wanted to kill you after you talked on the operating table and we found out that you are Jewish."

"Jesus tells us to love our enemies and to do good to those who persecute us," I answered. "He loved even those who drove Him to the cross, and he begged His Father's forgiveness for them."

Miss Grete's grief was not just from the physical assault she had suffered; it came from the broken vision of the glorious Fatherland, the realization that Hitler, the pied piper she had followed, was a fraud. The Third Reich had finally caused her pain—in its fall.

(Anita Dittman lives in Minnesota. Anyone interested in purchasing a copy of her entire book should contact Chad A. Filley at (218) 456-2516 or by e-mail chadfilley@rrv.net)

Anniversary
By
Chad A. Filley

(This is the only fictional short story included in the book. All characters represented in the story are completely fictional and should not be confused with anyone living or dead in the past or present. Any such incident would be purely coincidental.)

"Hello," the startled woman said. She had just discovered an intruder in her room as she awoke from a nap.
"Who are you?" she asked the friendly looking gray-haired man that stood before her holding a bouquet of flowers.
"I'm your husband, Otis, and I've brought you some flowers," he said in a calm tone trying to avoid upsetting her further.
"Who are you really?" Eleanor asked again. "Tell me or I'll call the nurses."
"It's Otis," he said. "I've brought you some pretty flowers to celebrate the 63rd anniversary of our first date. It's a bouquet of daisies just like the ones I brought to your house on our first date."
"I can't believe you are my husband," she said. "Why would a twenty-one-year-old like myself marry an old man like you?"

"You're not twenty-one. You live in a retirement home."

Otis' previous optimism that today might be one of Eleanor's better days was now gone. He put the flowers in the crystal vase on her dresser and sat down in the chair next to her bed.

"Who brought the nice flowers?"

"I did honey. It's our anniversary."

"Anniversary of what?"

"Our first date," Otis patiently explained. "Remember? We went on a double date picnic with your cousin Jim and your best friend Millie Perkins. We ate a picnic lunch out at Lake Esmerelda."

"Tell me more about this picnic," she asked.

Otis let out a deep sigh and began to think of the details.

"Your cousin Jim and I had been working in the hot fields helping your uncle Zeke with the haying, " Otis said. "Jim wanted to go out with Millie but she wouldn't go out on a date with him unless he could find a date for his cousin, Eleanor..."

"Who was his cousin?"

"It was you," Otis said. "But I hadn't met you yet. After quite a bit of coaxing, Jim finally talked me into going on the double date. I was pretty shy back then and you were probably the most beautiful girl that I had ever seen."

"I thought you said we hadn't ever met?"

"Jim showed me plenty of pictures," Otis said. "Anyway I showed up at your front porch with a bouquet of daisies..."

"I'm pleased to make your acquaintance Mr. Johanssen," the auburn-haired, fair-skinned young Eleanor Tavist said.

"Please call me Otis. I hope you like daisies." Otis couldn't believe his luck. She was probably the most beautiful sight he had ever set his eyes on. She was much prettier than Cindy Lawton, the girl that was crowned as last year's Miss Bluefield and had even gone on to win third place in the State Beauty Pageant.

"I much prefer roses, but these are very pretty," Eleanor said. "I must find a vase to put them in so they stay fresh."

No sooner had Eleanor ran into the house than Jim began honking the horn of his automobile. He rolled down his window and began yelling at Otis.

"Did you scare her away?"

"No, she wanted to put the flowers in a vase," Otis shouted back.

****

"I'd rather doubt you impressed me that much by bringing me daisies," Eleanor said interrupting his daydream. "I much prefer roses."

"Let me prove it to you," Otis said. "Pick up the Bible on the night stand next to your bed and open it to the book of Psalms."

Eleanor opened the sacred book and immediately found the remains of an ancient daisy that had been pressed between the books pages to remain a keepsake.

"You kept that daisy to remind yourself of our special day," Otis said.

"Were we engaged very long?"

"We dated for eighteen months. Your father said we had to wait until you graduated from high school before we could get married."

"Did we have any children?"

"We had one boy," Otis explained. "His name was Jimmy, named him after your cousin Jim."

"We only had one child? I'd rather doubt that because I love children and I certainly would have wanted to have had more children than that."

"Something happened to Jimmy..."

****

Eleanor commented to Otis that she couldn't believe her luck, it was half past six and not even a whimper had come from the nursery. It was the first time that little Jimmy had slept through the entire night without a fuss. Like any other mother she obediently answered her child's call, but she had a touch of the flu and was grateful that he had chosen tonight to sleep without interruption. Otis sat in bed and watched his lovely vision of a wife head towards the nursery to check on their three-month-old.

"Otis, come here!"

"What?" he shouted from the bed.

"It's Jimmy. I can't wake him!"

"What?"

"Come here. I can't wake him!"

As he rushed into the room he could see Jimmy's cute little body curled up as he lay on his tummy. As he reached over to pick him up his body was instantly overtaken by an indescribable chill. Instead of feeling a warm, full-of-life body, he was greeted with the ice-cold shell of what was once her alive son.

"Jimmy's gone!" Eleanor screamed. " I never should have slept through the night! It's all my fault!"

During the next few months Eleanor went into a shell. Some said she was just depressed while many others thought she should have been committed to the State Hospital in the Capital City.

Slowly she began to allow Otis back into her life, but things were never quite the same. She never quite forgave herself for not checking on Jimmy and she convinced Otis that having another child would just be too traumatic.

****

Eleanor began to cry.

"You mean something's happened to Jimmy! Bring him here right now. Oh my God! My baby! Jimmy!"

"Calm down dear," Otis said. "Jimmy's sleeping right now."

Slowly Eleanor began to calm down.

"Let him sleep for awhile and we'll wake him later," Otis said trying to pacify her.

A nurse walked in the room.

"Is everything okay in here?"

"Quiet. You need to be quiet or you'll wake the baby," Eleanor said in a scolding whisper.

"Sorry," the nurse said as she backed out of the room. The nurse couldn't bear to look at Otis when Eleanor was like this; it overwhelmed her with pity. She also knew better than to agitate Eleanor when she was reliving her short stint of motherhood.

"I just wanted to wish you a happy anniversary and I wanted to tell you some things that I've probably never told you before."

"Like what?"

"Well, I wanted you to know that you were the only woman I've ever loved and I wish that we could have had a whole house full of children..."

"Isn't Jimmy enough?"

"I guess you're right, he was enough," Otis said. "Anyway I just wanted to let you know that I wouldn't change a thing about my life unless it would have made you happier or it would have allowed me to spend more time with you."

"Did we always live in Bluefield?"

****

Otis rushed into the house, *"Honey, you'll never guess what. Company headquarters called and they want to transfer me to Holdingford."* He was beaming from ear to ear.

"They offered to pay all of our moving expenses plus double my salary. It will be great. Holdingford is the biggest grossing store in the state. It has a sales force of forty full-time men."

"We can't go to Holdingford," she said. "How can you even think of leaving Jimmy?"

"We wouldn't be leaving Jimmy," he said. "We can always come back and visit him at the cemetery."

"You can go, but it will be alone."

Otis had already turned down several promotions within the company. He knew that if he turned this one down too it was career suicide. He would probably never be offered another chance at a promotion. If he wanted to advance he had to leave Bluefield.

"I've seen the families that leave their loved ones and before you know it the visits become less and less frequent. Eventually they stop all together. I will never do that to our son."

"You're right dear. I don't know what I was thinking," he said knowing that he would never be able to reach his career goals from this moment on.

****

"I had many offers to leave Bluefield and make much more money, but I knew that it would make you happier to stay here, so I did."

"Bluefield is a nice town isn't it?"

Otis simply nodded his head.

"I guess what I'm trying to say is that I never wanted anything more than to make you happy and I tried my best. I really did."

"I am happy," Eleanor said. "I've got a great husband and a wonderful baby boy. Someday I'll have to introduce you to them."

"I just wanted to let you know that I get lonely sometimes and I really miss you. There are plenty of those blue-haired old hens that drop by with food, but they're no better than buzzards going after a freshly killed animal." Otis grabbed her hand and began stroking it. "I just miss the way things were. I'd give anything to have them back the way they were."

"I know what you mean," Eleanor said. "I went grocery shopping yesterday and they wanted more than 50 cents a gallon for milk. Imagine that. Where have the good old days gone?"

"I also hope that you can forgive me if I've ever hurt you in any way. You know that I would never have intentionally done anything to hurt you."

Otis leaned forward and gave her a light, tender kiss on the forehead.

"I hope that you don't regret anything about our lives together. I know I sure don't," he said as he turned to walk out the door.

****

"*I don't regret a thing Otis,*" she said. "*Thanks for 63 great years. I love you.*"

****

Otis almost fell over. He couldn't believe his ears. It had been two years since she suffered her first in a series of many strokes and this was the first time in many months that she had been able to communicate any knowledge of the present day.

He turned around to greet his returned companion when she blurted out "Do I know you?"

"Yes," Otis said unsuccessfully trying to fight back the tears. "We used to be very close."

He then took one final look at the colorful bouquet of daisies and walked out the door.

(Anniversary is one in a series of short stories Chad Filley has written about the fictitious town of Bluefield)

The Outsider
By
Chad A. Filley

Being an easy sell, some of the students knew that I probably wouldn't turn them down if they asked me to chaperone the high school dance following the football game.

Chaperoning a dance can be quite an interesting experience. It allows the chance to see all types of kids that are in many different phases of their life. There are the popular kids that are constantly dancing. There is the group of boys standing in the corner making fun of everyone that is dancing although they secretly long to be out there too. There are the girls that just came to have a good time and don't care what others think. They will even go out on the dance floor with a group of their girlfriends.

One of the other chaperones commented about a couple of the students that were being loud and obnoxious. They were overcompensating for their obvious feelings that they didn't fit in.

"I wonder if they came her tonight hoping that tonight might be different than all the other nights. I wonder if they came here hoping that maybe tonight they might actually fit in," he said. "Maybe when they were getting ready I wonder if they thought tonight might be their chance."

This chaperone's piercing comments really hit me. It brought me back to an incident that I hadn't thought of for several years. It brought me back to the days I worked as a youth minister.

One of my goals as a youth minister was to get as many youth from our congregation as possible to attend Bible camp. Sending a large number of youth to the camp gave me the excuse to spend the week with them and have the chance to behave like I was an adolescent once again.

Camp has a great deal to offer kids including swimming, hiking, bible studies, meeting youth from other towns that share the same values, singing campfire songs, hanging out with cool almost hero-like counselors, learning new crafts and participating in many fun games.

Campers are also given the chance to thrive in a non-threatening, put-down free atmosphere. These steadfast rules of camp are open to everyone unless you are like Pat.

I first encountered Pat while the campers were participating in the opening evening large group mixers. To be completely honest I was unsure whether Pat was a boy or a girl. Pat's clothing was gender neutral and his or her walk and hairstyle didn't lend a hint to an unsure observer. I asked one of the pastors that was also spending the week at camp whether he could tell and he couldn't help me out either.

Pat's lack of athletic skills was obvious to anyone even halfway observing the activities. Some of the older boys had taken it upon themselves to cheer for Pat. The cheering was done in the sneaky, covert way many adolescents use to taunt an outsider. Although Pat acted as if the cheers were appreciated it was obvious that the extra attention was a great deal more humiliating than encouraging.

After Pat was finally eliminated in the game I took the time to go over and offer a little encouragement.

"Way to go Pat," I said. "You did a nice job."

"Very funny mister," the blond-haired youth shot back at me. Pat's high-pitched voice did nothing to offer a hint to the owners gender.

"I'm serious Pat, you did a nice job..."

"My name's not Pat! It's Frederick."

"Why is everyone calling you Pat?"

"I don't know," Frederick said. "They have been ever since we got here."

"I meant what I said. You did a nice job out there, FREDERICK."

That evening before the campfire I stopped Darren, one of the older boys from my church, and asked him why everybody had been calling the unfortunate boy Pat.

"At first nobody could tell whether he was a boy or a girl, so we started calling him Pat. You know like the Pat on Saturday Night Live. Nobody can ever tell if it is a boy or a girl. He's really a nerd," Darren said.

I had seen the Pat skits and they were funny. I guess part of the reason the skits were funny is that there are actually people out there like the character being portrayed. I guess when the character is on television then it's okay, but it's not funny when the subject is a thirteen-year-old boy that is just trying to fit in.

"Do me a favor and lay off the name calling for awhile," I said. "His name is Frederick."

Darren's revelation hit me in the stomach with more force than any wrecking ball could have. I can't honestly say that I was completely empathetic to Frederick's dilemma, but I did hurt for him. Having an eighteen-month-old son back at home I couldn't help but think how terrible I, as a parent, would have felt if my son had been receiving the treatment Frederick was. These paternalistic feelings were something new to me. I'm not sure someone without children could have had the newfound guilt feelings that I had just encountered.

I can remember people telling me that parenting was going to open up a whole new world, but I never could have imagined how my entire perspective of certain events could have changed after the birth of an eight-pound baby boy.

Upon investigating I discovered that Frederick's congregation was hoping that this one-week at camp was going to offer him a refuge.

The next morning I approached several of the boys in Frederick's cabin and explained to them how rotten I would feel if they were treating my son like they treated Frederick. I then asked them how they would feel if it were their son that was being treated that way. Somehow I touched these boys on some sort of a deeper level and they not only began to treat Frederick better but they became his protectors. For the rest of the week they took it on as their duty to make sure he had a more positive experience.

Initially Frederick was very defensive to the kindness offered by the boys. Years of being teased had conditioned him to respond to other kids in a defensive manner. After awhile he loosened up and began to enjoy the attention from the others.

It would be great to be able to say that this week was a pivotal one in which Frederick's entire life was changed for the better, but I can't say that for sure. The one thing I can say is that Frederick's week long experience at Bible Camp was probably one of the best weeks of his life.

Whatever It Takes

(An experience in the life of Glen, Julie and Carol Brookshire as told to Chad Filley)

    It started out like any other Monday morning. Glen Brookshire left early for work because he had to help set up for a banquet that evening. He never thought twice about heading to work.

    He had no sooner arrived at work when his wife Julie called to tell him to come home because their thirteen-month-old daughter, Carol, had quit breathing. Her little body was convulsing.

    Glen immediately left for home, but it was no easy task to reach his home which was located four miles outside of Marion, Indiana. He had to drive through nearly impassable roads that were covered with a fresh coat of wet Indiana snow. Knowing his pickup wouldn't make it on the roads he headed into a field to see if he could make it, but he got stuck.

    A Good Samaritan with a four-wheel drive got him home despite the snowy conditions.

    After entering the house Glen immediately saw Julie holding their young daughter who was convulsing. He then called the police to ask for help, but eventually ended up heading back to town along a different route. The Good Samaritan had assembled a group of his friends and they traveled back to town in a four-wheel drive convoy.

After arriving at the hospital in Marion they went to an exam room.

We got into the room and she went limp while we were waiting," Glen said. "She was completely unconscious."

He ran out into the hallway and got an orderly and told him to get a doctor immediately.

The doctor came in and he didn't have a clue about what he was dealing with. He asked all kinds of questions regarding what she had eaten. They couldn't think of anything that could have caused this.

The doctor had just seen her the Wednesday before to treat her for pink eye, and he couldn't think of any reason she could be like this. The doctor finally decided to admit her to the hospital and she was initially taken to isolation.

The Brookshire's sister-in-law, Jean Ann, worked at the hospital. She had gotten a call from Glen's mother and went down during her break to see how Carol was doing.

"We thought Carol had died," Glen said. "People were running in and out of the room, and we could hear them calling out codes."

"By this time they had started mouth-to-mouth resuscitation," Julie said.

The medical team took her to the elevator to get her to the intensive care unit to hook her up to a respirator.

"She was in seizures the whole time," Julie said.

The doctor suspected Reye's syndrome, but he had no proof. In 1979 they didn't know that much about the disease. They continued to run all kinds of tests on Carol as they searched for answers.

It was decided that they should transport her to the Indiana Medical Center in Indianapolis. Julie and Jean Ann went down with Carol in the ambulance.

"She died at least three times on the way to Indianapolis," they explained. "Our sister-in-law brought her back each time."

The battery for the respirator didn't work in the ambulance, so Jean Ann had to do mouth-to-mouth the entire way there.

Glen stayed back to make arrangements for their two other children, seven-year-old Donna and five-year-old Jason.

It was about five o'clock in the afternoon when they arrived at the Indiana Medical Center. Upon arriving they were ready to treat her for Reye's syndrome, but she didn't have the right symptoms.

"They didn't know what to do," Julie said, "so they admitted her."

They asked all kinds of family history questions. They examined her for meningitis, but they couldn't come up with anything. It wasn't uncommon for people with Reye's to be misdiagnosed. While they were at the hospital there was a teenage girl brought in to the emergency room that was very sick. The doctor felt she had been taking drugs and sent her home with her parents. They ended up taking her back and it was later discovered that she had Reye's syndrome. The only long-lasting complication she suffered was that her voice changed.

"They kept saying they didn't know what was going on. She didn't have the right symptoms for Reye's syndrome," Julie told.

After making all the necessary plans Glen finally arrived in Indianapolis. Julie hadn't seen Carol since they brought her in. Glen went up to the counter and demanded to see his daughter immediately.

Glen and Julie were brought up to the room to see her, and they could see numerous people working on her.

"It took them three days to diagnose her," Julie said.

During that time they had narrowed it down to Reye's or herpes. They explained that they could treat herpes, but not Reye's syndrome. When they asked what the treatment for herpes was they were told they didn't even want to know. The doctor's told them it was much worse than the disease.

"They did it with a liver biopsy," Glen said explaining how they finally made the correct diagnosis.

The Brookshire's spent the next three-and-a-half weeks in the children's intensive care unit waiting room.

"They let us visit her for five minutes every hour on the hour," Glen explained.

When they visited their daughter they saw her naked body in a cast that kept her immobile. She also had a probe between the brain and the skull, tubes in her arms and legs, and a monitor hooked up to her body. She was also in a perpetual barbiturate coma to put her body in a condition to where it could be controlled.

"We didn't know from one hour to the next if she was going to make it," Glen said.

"The doctor's kept telling us she's on a tightrope. They said they didn't know which way she was going," Julie said. "I felt sorry for the doctors because they thought she was going to die."

One doctor even avoided Julie in the hall because it bothered him so much that there was nothing they could do about it.

Family members were beginning to worry about what they would do with Julie if Carol did die. They knew she wouldn't accept the fact that it could happen.

Glen and Julie slept on the waiting room chairs for the next five weeks. During the time Carol spent in the hospital, fourteen other children had contracted the syndrome.

One night at two a.m. Glen woke up and went to see Carol. The nurse stopped him on the way in to the room to tell him that she probably wasn't going to make it much longer. Not knowing whether he should wake Julie up he decided to go for a walk.

He went down the elevator and went outside. Overwhelmed by anger Glen punched a brick wall causing his knuckles to instantly become skinned up.

"God if you give her back to me," Glen pleaded. "I'll do whatever it takes. Just give her back to me."

Glen took the several minutes to clear his head and then decided to go back up to the room to check on Carol. During that time, which was only about a half hour, the nurse had done something, and upon seeing Glen she informed him that "Carol's doing much better now."

"From that moment on," Glen said, "I knew she was going to make it."

Julie felt that she had known this all along. She often had a recurring dream as she slept in the waiting room chair she had claimed stake to.

This dream included a vision of Carol being held in a large pair of hands. This recurring dream offered Julie many peaceful nights' rest.

"Whenever I saw these hands," Julie said, "I knew that Carol was going to be okay."

Carol was the youngest known survivor from Reye's Syndrome, but her challenges were far from over. The next months dealt with maintenance on her tracheotomy and nursing a horrible bedsore that actually exposed her tailbone.

The nurses and doctors knew that although Carol was going to live she wasn't ever going to be the same. When they finally sat Glen and Julie down to tell them that she had severe brain damage neither one of them had a clue how serious her condition was.

Sometime after her release from the hospital the Brookshire's moved to Minnesota.

"It was a year later before we realized how badly the brain had been damaged," Julie said. After several seizures they brought Carol to Minneapolis to have a CAT scan and when they saw the picture of her brain they knew how severe her condition really was.

"The whole brain was damaged," Julie said.

"The first thing people began to ask us was where we wanted her placed," Glen said. Having made a promise that he would do whatever it takes, putting her in nursing care was never an option.

"I don't blame others for doing it," he said, "but it was never an option for us."

Initially Glen and Julie would grind up food for Carol to eat, but it was later found out that some of the food was going into her lungs causing her to cough. After finding this out it was decided that they should put a feeding tube in her stomach.

Carol also had metal bars put into her spine to combat scoliosis. These bars prevent her spine from pushing into her lungs. She is wheelchair bound and cortically deaf and blind. Her brain doesn't translate symbols.

"Many people told us early on that this could break us up," Julie said. "We made up our mind that it wouldn't hurt us. It actually made us better."

"Whatever it takes," said Glen reinforcing his wife's comment.

There was a period of time when the two had to care for Carol every two hours around the clock.

"We never looked at this as a sacrifice," Glen said. "It's just something you do."

"We did make a conscious decision to never let it interfere with our two other children," Julie said. They had a system worked out that one or the other would attend all school activities.

"The only events that we attended together were their high school graduations," Glen said.

The Brookshire's gave up many things that most people take for granted. They weren't able to take summer vacations or do things like go camping at the lakes like many Minnesotans do every weekend.

"You have to keep things in perspective," Glen said. "There's always somebody out there that has it a little tougher than we do."

Every day Glen and Julie live up to their end of the bargain. The way they look at it they are simply doing "Whatever it takes."

Glen, Julie and Carol reside in Halstad, Minnesota. Glen has been the mayor of Halstad for several years.

The Decision

(An incident that occurred during Carol Brookshire's hospitalization)

Often when people are faced with a crisis of their own they are able to help others out by ministering to them.

"We were much better off than many of the people we met during our six weeks," Glen Brookshire said. Glen and his wife, Julie, had struck up an impromptu support group with many of the other parents of sick children. Unfortunately they witnessed several parents' last moments with their children.

One couple brought their six-week-old child in and nobody could figure out what was wrong. The baby's conditions kept deteriorating and eventually they flew in some mice to do testing with. After doing the testing the mouse died and they found out the mother had contracted toxoplasmosis.

During one of Glen's sleepless nights he walked out into the hallway to get some fresh air. There was a window at the end of one of the secluded hallways in which the window could be opened.

As Glen headed down the hallway he noticed a man sitting in front of the window.

Glen asked the man how he was doing and the man instantly broke down in tears. The man explained that his five-year-old daughter had been playing on a swing set and had fallen off and hit her head.

"The only reason she's alive," the man told Glen, "is because she's hooked up to a machine."

The doctor's had told the man and his wife that they needed to make a decision whether or not they were going to pull the plug on her respirator.

The man told Glen that his wife wouldn't make the decision so she left it up to him. He was sitting there trying to decide what to do.

The two men began swapping stories about themselves and talked up until morning. Eventually the man asked Glen what he would do if he were in his situation.

This was a tough dilemma for Glen to face. With his thirteen-month-old daughter in serious condition he knew that he too might be confronted with this decision.

"I don't know," he said, "but I think I would pull the plug."

After talking some more the man went down and told his wife that he was going to do this. All of the little girl's family members were allowed in one by one to say goodbye to the little girl.

The father was the last one in the room. Glen was waiting out in the hallway when he finally came out.

"That was a tough one," Glen said. "I still didn't know at that time if I'd have to do that myself."

"To this day I don't know how he found the strength to do that," he said.

Two Steps Short of a Mile

As told by Judy Siegle

Judy Siegle was the leader of the pack during her high school years. She sang in the choir, played in the band, ran track and was a member of the speech team. Although successful in all of these activities her true passion was displayed as she excelled on the basketball court. Siegle was named to the all conference team three times and made the Minnesota all-state team following her senior season.

Upon graduating from high school in 1979 Judy planned to attend Concordia College in Moorhead, Minnesota, and continue her basketball-playing career.

Her plans came to a screeching halt on August 11, 1979. Just weeks away from her freshman year at the small Lutheran college, Judy was involved in a horrible car accident. She had suffered a spinal cord injury which eventually left her an incomplete quadriplegic.

"I was in and out of consciousness for about a week," Judy said. She was initially unable to recall any of the events surrounding the accident. "I gradually became aware of what happened."

Almost instantly Judy felt no real reason or need to grieve. She felt that if God was always with her, then this was okay.

"I felt that if God could better use me from a wheelchair then that's where I should be," she said adding, "I had no way of comprehending how my life would change."

She received terrific hometown support from friends and family in Pelican Rapids, Minnesota, and she also benefited from a great wealth of support from the student body at Concordia College. Members of the women's basketball team visited her in the hospital and the football team presented her with the game ball from the opening game that fall.

The events of the accident were gradually revealed to her through scattered memories. She also began to suffer from nightmares and many restless nights.

One morning while she was working with her occupational therapist she heard the Concordia Chapel on the radio. She immediately began to think about not being able to attend college and not being a part of the women's basketball team. She began to cry.

"I had realized that many of the things I had been working for weren't going to happen," Judy said.

The occupational therapist turned the radio off and began talking with Judy.

Judy then called Concordia's chaplain, Ernie Mancini, to see if they could possibly meet to discuss her feelings. He came over that evening to talk with her.

"Ernie told me that there were going to be many more times when I would be hurt," she said. " He told me that believing in God didn't mean I wouldn't experience bouts of frustration and anger."

He also helped her combat the nightmares. Mancini told her to imagine that God was so close to her that she could beat his chest. She took his advice and it helped to end her nightmares.

"After that I realized that I would hurt along the way, but God was going with me," she said. "I felt a great deal of peace with that."

Judy spent three months in a Fargo hospital and then spent the next three months rehabilitating in Denver.

Judy never accepted the fact that she wouldn't return to her pre-accident form. Combining partial return of her legs with her strong work ethic and prior athletic experiences, she became more and more determined to push herself to once again walk.

"I knew how to push my body," she said. "I didn't know what was possible, so I pushed my body to walk."

After three months in Denver (six months after the accident) she walked off an airplane at Fargo's Hector Airport with a walker and leg braces. She then built a workout into her daily routine with the focus on walking. At that time she knew nothing about disabled sports.

During the fall of 1980 she began attending Concordia. Judy felt as if life was getting back to normal for her. She took a normal load of classes, lived in the freshman dorm, worked out daily and had a boyfriend back home.

"I didn't see myself as being that different than anybody else," she said. "Instead of limiting myself I tried to focus on the possibilities."

Although Judy attacked things with a positive attitude there were things that got her down.

"You don't grieve a disability once and for all at a certain point in time," she explained, "You grieve different things at different times."

During freshman orientation Judy wasn't able to participate when the other students went to the park to play games.

"I went to the dorm room and cried," she said, "It hurt me that I couldn't participate in the way I could have a year before."

Through these times Judy learned to be open with God.

"I knew that I needed a wheelchair as a means of mobility," she said, "but I also knew that it didn't mean I was less of a person."

Judy had gone from being one of the most active leaders in high school to someone who was outside the circle at college. She came to the realization that this was okay, and that she was of no less value then she had been before.

Every day Judy would work out with leg braces and a walker. These workouts consisted of her walking in Concordia's field house. Walking was no easy task for her. She had to step forward with one leg and then swing the other one in order to move. She continually prayed for good workouts.

Each day Judy kept pushing herself hoping that she would be able to walk on her own again. Nobody could tell her with absolute certainty that this wouldn't be possible.

"I thought it might take me some time, but I thought I was going to do it," she said.

During the last day of school of her freshman year Judy decided to get a workout in before going home for the summer.

"I thought I'd get in one quick lap," she explained, "and get my workout in."

She began to walk with her leg braces and walker and then something happened. Her legs began striding out with no effort.

"I thought this was it," she said. "I thought I'd been healed."

Instantly she began to think of whom she should go to tell first. It felt so good that she continued to walk.

While walking she began to think of ways to thank God. She began reciting in her mind Bible verses she had learned in Sunday school and singing camp songs she had learned during her days as a youth at Bible Camp.

Up until that day Judy hadn't ever walked more than five laps. Before she knew it she was on lap eight. She then decided she wanted to do a mile (twelve full laps).

"I can remember my back beginning to get tired, and I could feel my hands squishing with blisters from putting some weight on the walker," she said, adding that after hitting the eleventh lap she was determined to make it all the way. "I really wanted to make the mile. Having been an athlete the mile was a mark of excellence that I knew all so well."

Judy was just two steps short of her electric wheelchair when she lost her balance and fell; just two steps short of her goal.

A couple of faculty members from the college that were playing a game of pickup basketball rushed over to help her up. By this time Judy had tears flowing down her cheeks.

"That morning walking a mile was the furthest thing from my mind," she said, "It thrilled me to know that the power to walk came from somewhere outside me."

Judy felt that God was talking to her through her actions. He was telling her that he was with her all of the way, and that her falling revealed that she couldn't do it without him.

"He was telling me that I'm not there yet, but he'll be with me all the way."

Judy knows that there will come a day when she is able to run and jump and skip.

"It may not come in this lifetime, but it will come," she said.

Judy drove her wheelchair immediately to tell Ernie Mancini. She showed him the blisters on her hands and told him what happened.

The next day she was excited to see how the walking would go, but her pace was back to a slow effortful pace.

The next year in a religion class an instructor gave the definition of a miracle.

"It's not just an astounding event," the instructor explained, "but one that reveals God in a certain way."

These words rang true for Judy. This miracle had revealed God in her life in a whole way.

"This turned on a light bulb for me. It told me that my experience was a miracle and that God was going with me," she said. "His power would put me where I needed to be so I could to do what I needed to do."

She also came to the realization that the miracles in the Bible are not only encouraging for the person they happen to, but also to all that see or hear about them.

Judy realized that God wasn't through with her yet. She tried her hand at wheelchair basketball, but her triceps weren't strong enough to be able to get the ball into the basket. Eventually she became involved in quad rugby, which she humbly claims she wasn't very good at. Despite her claims the team was good enough to qualify for the national tournaments in San Jose.

While at the national tournaments she found out about wheelchair road racing. She got her own racing chair, began participating in races and the athlete in her came out again.

Being a quadriplegic she was at a disadvantage when racing against paraplegics. (Quadriplegic's have suffered a broken neck while a paraplegic is paralyzed from the waist down.) She was told she would have to compete at the national level to be on a level playing field with other quads.

She contacted the University of Illinois in Champaign-Urbana to inquire about training with their wheelers, some of the best in the country and ended up going to Illinois for a racing clinic.

During the clinic the presenters individually evaluated the form of the wheelchair racers. Over the course of the evening Judy was evaluated and told that she had room to improve in many different areas if she was going to be successful.

"I went back to my room more than a little discouraged," she admitted.

No longer sure if she wanted to do this anymore, she remembered back to her college days when she'd dared to step out and take a risk.

"I knew I had to try," she said, "whether I made the paralympic team or not. I knew it would be a positive experience."

Judy prayed to God not knowing what his plans for her were.

She asked God "If this is your plan than please put the supports along the way to make things happen."

Things did happen and people helped her along the way. Judy received the needed help from different coaches and even a bike shop mechanic who helped her with wheelchair maintenance.

"It would have been too overwhelming to do it alone," she said.

Judy has since set many national records. She currently holds records in the 400, 800, 1500 and 5000-meter events, has participated in the 1996 paralympics in Atlanta and earned medals in the Pan American Games. She is currently training for the 2000 paralympics in Sydney, Australia.

Judy is quick to praise God for all of her successes. She also knows that a great deal of her success goes back to the day in the field house when she miraculously ended up falling two steps short of a mile.

Judy has received numerous awards including North Dakota's Outstanding Citizen 1990 and Minnesota State High School League Hall of Fame member 1999.

Judy is an excellent motivational speaker with inspiring presentation topics. Anyone interested in contacting her for a speaking engagement can contact her by mail at:
    Judy Siegle
    620 Main
    Apt. # 405
    Fargo, ND 58103

You Don't Know What You Have Until You Almost Lose It
By
Chad A. Filley

Our family decided to combat the winter blues by spending a weekend at a hotel with a swimming pool. Although this may sound like it was a good idea this so-called vacation turned out to be anything but relaxing.

Our two oldest sons (Trent and Tyrel) constantly fought with one another as most eight and four year olds do. Our youngest son added to the stress level by howling anytime that he was taken more than ten feet away from the baby pool. Since he was just a little over a year old he required a continual watchful eye. By the end of the weekend my wife, Candy, and I were getting quite edgy. Our great idea had turned into much more stress than it was worth.

Often times when things got stressful I seem to revert back to either thinking about the good old days when it was just Candy and I or thinking ahead to the days when the boys will be grown up and we will once again have the house to ourselves. I know I'm not alone because I've heard other parents share the same sentiments.

There were times when I, as a young father, wondered why things couldn't be perfect like a Norman Rockwell painting or the television shows of the fifties. I often wondered what it would be like to have children that didn't embarrass me every single time we went out in public.

    I was about to really get going on my "poor me" bandwagon when I remembered a time when I had felt this way and I soon discovered life wouldn't smell like roses without my family intact.

    A couple of years earlier Candy, Trent, Tyrel and I headed to the local Wal-Mart to pick up a few items. During the fifteen-minute commute to the store we had faced several minor crises and two minor altercations between the boys. We also stopped to eat dinner which was usually anything but uneventful.

    By the time I arrived at the store I'm certain that if a wish-granting genie had offered to exchange my children in for some better behaved pit bulls I probably would have taken him up on it.

    Immediately after entering the store we grabbed a shopping cart and headed toward the jewelry department in search of a new battery for my watch. After finding the needed battery the clerk offered to install it for us while we continued to shop.

    As we began looking around Candy noticed the spinning display rack of sunglasses.

    "Let's see if we can find a pair for Tyrel," she said launching into a dissertation about how it was next to impossible to find a pair that wouldn't fall off of our eighteen-month-olds small, round nose.

After trying on several pairs she actually discovered a pair that fit perfectly. She then slid them into the cart without him noticing and proceeded on to look for needed toiletries. Knowing where she was going I would willingly offer to do just about anything to avoid the ritual of strolling down the shampoo and toilet paper aisles. To avoid this torturous activity I offered to keep the boys with me as I browsed around the book and electronics sections.

This in itself doesn't sound too bad unless you know my sons. Trent, then a kindergartner, wasn't too tough to handle, but Tyrel could euphemistically be described as full of energy. It wasn't unusual for Tyrel to stand up in or even jump off of a cart while it was in motion. One time he had jumped off the cart onto a stack of cereal boxes causing the entire stack to come crashing to the ground. Things had gotten so bad with our little daredevil that we had jokingly discussed tying his shoes together as he sat in the seat in hope of preventing him from being able to stand up.

Trent asked if he could go around the corner to look at the flip chart of posters while Tyrel held onto my hand. I momentarily let go of his hand to place the book I had been looking at back on the shelf, and when I turned to look at him he was gone!

Initially I wasn't too excited because I figured he had just gone around the corner to look at posters with his brother, but when I walked around the corner he was nowhere to be found.

"Where's your brother?"

"I don't know," Trent said not even looking away from the posters.

Instantly I went from being calm, cool and collected to a nervous wreck. Numerous horrifying scenarios immediately began shooting through my mind.

I grabbed Trent's hand as we combed through the aisles in search of Tyrel. All the time I became more and more paranoid that something bad had happened to him. I began to think of all of the horror stories I had heard about missing children never to be seen again. All I could think about was how much I wanted to see him again.

I had quickly learned that you never really know what you have until you lose it. How could this have happened? I had only let go of his hand for a second and poof he was gone. It was like some sort of magic trick gone badly.

After a couple of minutes of searching Trent and I ran into Candy.

"Where's Tyrel?" she asked.

I didn't know what to say and how to say it. Imagine trying to tell your normally forgiving spouse that you had lost your child.

"He's lost. I can't find him," I said as my wife's face turned from a nice tan color to an unusually milky white tone as she listened to my words.

"You find him, NOW!"

The three of us walked together for another couple of minutes when an employee broke in over the loudspeaker.

"May I have your attention please. We have some lost parents. There's a little blonde haired boy waiting for his lost parents at the courtesy counter..."

"Go get him," Candy said.

As I walked through the store, nearly in tears, I couldn't help but be grateful, but I was also filled with shame and embarrassment. How could I have lost my child?

As I approached the courtesy desk the clerk handed him to me before I could even say a word. He wrapped his arms around my neck giving me a big bear hug.

"I can see by the look on your face that you must be his father," she said.

"Thank you very much," I said hoping to convey just how appreciative I really was. "By the way where did you find him?"

"He was right here at the front door. He would have gotten outside too, but he was pushing on the "in" doors," she explained.

I thanked her several more times and as I turned to head back to find Candy, the clerk asked me "Do you want these?"

I turned around to see what she was talking about as she handed me a pair of children's sunglasses. Then it all made sense. He had gone back to get a pair of the sunglasses and then navigated all the way to the front door. He was probably the world's youngest shoplifter and all I could do was laugh with joy.

    I later found out from a Wal-Mart employee that the first thing I should have done was notify a store employee and the store would shut down until the missing child was found. No one would be able to leave or enter the store until the child was safely back in the arms of his or her parents.

    While walking back to find Candy and Trent I hugged Tyrel a little tighter than usual.

    Remembering those horrible few moments has helped me make it through many of the trying incidents of parenthood. Occasional frustration and embarrassment is a small price to pay when the alternative is being without them. I also discovered the very valuable lesson that you don't know what you have until you almost lose it.

Hiroshima

As told by Ernie Mancini

I was a young pastor right out of seminary at Our Redeemer's Lutheran in Benson, Minnesota. I was the first youth pastor in the entire county in 1969 and almost by accident youth ministry kind of grew up around me and my home.

The kids in that area were enormously talented musically and by the end of that summer we had about 35 kids with guitars, bass guitars and drums learning to play some of the new contemporary Christian music. We also took a lot of the popular songs and rewrote the words.

I was asked to speak at Green Lake Bible Camp's final campfire. Instead of speaking I asked if I could bring the musical group, which we now called the Koinonians. Koinonian is a Greek word that means the family or the brotherhood and it just fit well with the turbulent period of 1969.

By the end of the first year we had 85 singers and had done around forty concerts all over the region including Minnesota, North Dakota, Wisconsin and even as far east as Chicago. We were singing before very large audiences and we were responded to in an overwhelming fashion because the time was right.

Times were difficult in 1969. The nation was challenged in many, many ways and the people responded well when they saw a group of young people with a message of hope presented with lively and powerful contemporary music. We even cut a record for RCA and it sold very well.

The second year we had grown even larger to about 100 singers. We had about 35 to 40 concerts, many of which were on television, and we also cut a second record. The third year we had 116 members, all from the Benson area, with a big instrumental accompaniment and an audio-visual backup. We had forty-some concerts that year and an invitation to the White House, which we actually ended up not accepting because something else came up. That "something else" revolves around the story I want to tell.

In November of 1971 some Japanese Lutheran pastors and some Japanese missionaries were back in the United States touring the country. We were invited to Dayton's (department store) to give a concert which was to be broadcast live on WCCO radio. The pastors happened to hear the concert back in their hotel rooms and they thought that this would be a wonderful way to witness to Japanese teenagers because of the contemporary style and the joyful power of the message.

Together in December they formulated an invitation for our group to go to Japan in June of 1972 and tour the largest concert halls. We would have to pay to get over there and they would pay all of the expenses while we were in Japan. We were going to be sponsored by the

Catholic and Lutheran Churches of Japan and by the Japanese Lions Club.

During the next six months we fundraised to meet the costs of transportation. Japanese people drove in from the Twin Cities to educate us in language, culture and history. We were booked in the largest concert halls and scheduled to be on national television and radio. It was far beyond any of our wildest dreams.

We left in early June on a chartered United Airlines Jet. We arrived in Tokyo after a 14-hour sleepless flight and were immediately brought to the largest television station in Japan. We rehearsed for about six hours at this station for a show the next night that was going to be seen by millions of Japanese people.

In our five days in Tokyo we were on national television three times, national radio two times and Far East radio once. Our first concert was at St. Mary's Cathedral, the largest Catholic facility in Tokyo, and we even sang in Tokyo's equivalence of Carnegie Hall in front of a packed audience.

Because of all that exposure in Tokyo all of the rest of the stops on the trip were sellouts. That's something we could never have hoped or prayed for. It just happened. One newspaper had a huge headline that read "Genki group from America comes to Japan". Genki meant enthusiastic or special.

This was significant because America was in Vietnam in 1972 and there was a great deal of anti-American sentiment. The article said that we were a group of Americans that seemed to love the Japanese and their culture.

Even though the trip was wonderful in many different ways we were all focused on one city on the trip. That city was Hiroshima.

We were to be the largest American group to appear at the famous Peace Memorial Auditorium, which is about 100 yards from ground zero in downtown Hiroshima.

The time had come after this incredible high that we entered Hiroshima for two days. The first day we would get in at one o'clock in the afternoon, do some sight seeing and then we would sing the concert on the second night.

The people of Benson thought this concert was so important that they worked up a telephone hookup so Benson's radio station (KBMO) could carry the last three numbers and interviews with me and five of the kids live on the air. They all wanted to find out what it was like being in Hiroshima.

Our Japanese hosts understood how we felt. They first took us to the Atomic Blast Memorial Museum right at ground zero. We were there for about three hours. We saw things there that still turn my stomach today (28 years later).

We saw unbelievable sights, unbelievable stories and unbelievable exhibits including pictures of people whose bones were fused into the concrete because of the heat of the blast. We witnessed what could happen in the twinkling of an eye when an atomic bomb is dropped, and of course, this has only happened twice in history.

During our three-hour visit we saw exhibit after exhibit and heard story after story each more horrifying than the one before.

    Our incredibly gracious Japanese hosts must have known what we would be feeling like and instead of having us stay in homes, like we did at most places, they put us up at this gorgeous Olympic training camp in the Hiroshiman Hills. It was a wonderful place with an Olympic size swimming pool. They must have understood that we would be feeling things even though we had all of those amenities. When we arrived there I knew we would be in trouble.

    I told my wife, who had come along on the trip, that I was going to sleep in the infirmary by myself because I knew what was going to happen and it did. The kids came to me all night long, most of them in tears.

    "I feel so guilty...I feel so bad...I can't face them anymore... I can't sing tomorrow night..." Of course none of these kids had even been born at the time of the war. The longest night that I can remember experiencing finally wound up to dawn and I had no idea how we were going to meet our commitment to sing.

    We got up that morning and ate what has to be the quietest breakfast involving 116 teenagers in the history of mankind. There wasn't a peep. I wondered what I was going to do.

    Our Japanese hosts were so wise. They put us in the buses and took us downtown Hiroshima and brought us into a beautiful cafeteria with brown tables.

We were then introduced to a speaker, the Reverend Kiyoshi Tanimoto, that changed everything. I had never heard of him before, but there is quite a bit of material devoted to him in John Hersey's book "Hiroshima". He was a Methodist pastor in a nation that is less than one-percent Christian.

He proceeded to tell us in his own words all the stories that happened the day "hell visited the earth". He was then a young man who lived in downtown Hiroshima. It was a beautiful morning and he went up into the hills to visit relatives. He was standing outside on the street overlooking Hiroshima when the sirens went off. That wasn't anything new because planes flew over all the time. He also knew the war would soon be over because the American forces were already in Guam and most felt a mainland invasion would soon be coming.

"We could never have conceived a particular bomb that could have done that," Tanimoto said.

As Tanimoto turned and walked down the street he suddenly felt the earth shake. He said the blast was so loud that people in Hiroshima didn't hear a thing, but people a hundred miles away heard it. He said that thankfully he wasn't looking downtown, but was looking away. There was an almost blinding flash of light followed by a tremor and an incredible wind that knocked him over while the streets shook. Then a black rain began to fall.

"I looked at my city and there was this awesome mushroom cloud and underneath it my city was gone," he said. "It was just gone."

Then he began to tell stories of people in his parish and the stories of relatives who were killed instantly in the most grotesque manners or who died slowly and painfully. He himself lost all of his hair (it eventually grew back). The people were incredibly devastated.

He told story after story, and when he was finished everyone in the room was sobbing. This very gentle man looked at our entire group and asked if anyone had any questions.

I didn't figure anyone in the room could even talk. One of the girls in the room, a high school junior from Benson, raised her hand and with her voice choking with emotion she asked the question that every one of us felt.

"Pastor Tanimoto, do you still hate us?"

A gasp went up in the room.

Pastor Tanimoto walked across the room through the tables to where she was. He picked her up out of her chair and hugged her. While he hugged her he turned to us and said, "There is something you must understand. Hiroshima is our fault. Hiroshima is my sin."

He continued by saying, "I am a Christian pastor and I knew what was going on in my country. I knew that the warring people were surrounding the emperor and forcing us to do things that we shouldn't have done, most of all to bomb Pearl Harbor. As a Christian pastor I knew the truth and I didn't effectively witness to the rest of the Japanese. My darling, Hiroshima is my fault. Hiroshima is my sin."

We were absolutely stunned, but it was healing. It was very, very healing.

That evening Peace Memorial Hall was packed. There were even people sitting in the aisles.

Pastor Tanimoto came out on the stage and addressed the huge crowd of Japanese teenagers.

"It's only by a miracle isn't it. Thirty years ago your fathers and these young people's fathers were locked in mortal combat over issues that none of us really understood. We killed each other by the hundreds of thousands and now because of the grace of Jesus Christ and that only you are here together. You are praising our Lord, learning about each other and embracing each other as brothers and sisters. Need I say anymore about the power of Jesus Christ and the love of these young Americans?"

The place erupted in applause as he introduced us. It was the best concert we had in the three and a half weeks. We were on national radio in Japan and were carried on KBMO in Benson.

From that time on I don't think any of us was left unchanged. I had a very different idea about war and peace and about what my responsibility as a Christian is. I need to take responsibility for my country and for myself. I think every one of those young Americans felt the same way. We can be proud of our country and thank God for our country, but we as Christians also have a gospel to preach that is above any national creed.

We learned to love people we had barely met, and we learned to share their pain as well as they share our message of a risen, loving and redemptive Lord.

Ernie is currently the Executive Director of Alumni Relations at Concordia College in Moorhead, Minnesota.

The Hug Quota
By
Pastor Jim Holthus

It was the first meeting of our morning Bible study for senior high students. We met at the church just across the street from the high school at 7 a.m. and I would furnish rolls, juice and milk to everyone that showed up. We had about a dozen youth that showed up a little sleepy-eyed but glad to be there and enjoy fellowship with one another.

First, the rolls and juice were sampled as they gathered. Second, we read the word together and shared ideas before a time of prayer. Just before we finished at 7:30 we stood and held hands and prayed the Lord's Prayer together. Then I mentioned the "hug quota."

I explained that scientists who study human behavior had learned that each person needed at least two hugs a day to be "okay." People who got 5 or 6 hugs a day were affirmed, enthusiastic and set for a few days while people who got a dozen or so hugs would feel great about themselves and would be ecstatic for a week or so. Then I suggested that we institute a kind of "hug quota" where we would try to give one another enough hugs at the end of our Bible studies so we could each make it through the week feeling loved and accepted.

As we began to hug one another, I realized that the extroverted kids were the ones going around the room giving hugs while the introverts were the youths that hesitantly stood in one place hoping that someone would come to them and offer a hug. No hugs were ever turned down. I was one of the extroverts giving hugs when I noticed something that made me feel awkward.

One introverted kid, who I'll call "Todd," stood by himself near the door of the church lounge. He was the kind of youth who always seems to be on the fringe despite desperately wanting to be part of the accepted crowd. Todd tried so hard to fit in everywhere and it always seemed to the other kids that he tried too hard.

When other kids were standing talking among themselves, Todd would come up and say, "Hi! What are you talking about?" and the conversation would basically stop. The youth didn't dislike Todd, they just felt awkward around him. Some of their discomfort was the fear that if they were nice and accepting to Todd that he would view them for a while as a best friend and follow him around at school, which might be embarrassing to the "normal" kids. So in spite of his best awkward efforts, Todd remained on the fringe, even here.

As I was giving hugs to the "normal" kids, I noticed him standing by the door of the lounge. His hands were halfway up and halfway open to receive a hug and his face had a kind of pleading look on it which seemed to say, "Hug me, Please."

Everyone else in the group was getting or giving hugs, but it seemed that we all counted on someone else to break the ice and hug Todd. He was the only one who hadn't given or received any hugs. This was as close as he could get to asking for a hug; he'd been rejected so many times before that he didn't dare risk being turned down again. If he were rejected here, at church youth group Bible study, would there ever be any one place where he could possibly be affirmed? So I disengaged myself from my current hug and began to move toward Todd to hug him, but I had waited too long before noticing him. His face seemed to fall as he lowered his hands and quickly hurried out the door and ran down the hall toward the exit. I cringed inside as I realized he was gone.

I felt very small as the "normal" kids left, each saying they had a good time and intended to come back next week before school. I sat down in the lounge wondering if this morning had done more harm than good, at least for one young man.

I struggled all week with myself, wondering what I could have done differently and wishing I'd have noticed Todd standing by the door earlier. I prayed that he'd come back next week and that I'd find a way to make it up to him. I knew I had to do something to let the group realize the same things I'd discovered at the end of the Bible study.

I decided to bring the rolls and juice into the lounge again but deliberately left the milk in the downstairs refrigerator of the church. I waited and prayed that Todd would appear and give us all another chance to be the "body of Christ" for one another. We were supposed to begin our Bible study shortly after 7 a.m. but I continued to wait. Even though we had many of the same kids who had been there last week, it was just after seven when Todd walked into the church lounge and quickly took a seat, almost as if he didn't want to be realized by anyone. I waited a few minutes and made small talk with many of the youth and the additional stragglers. Finally, I spoke.

"Todd, I think I forgot to bring the milk up from the basement. It's in the refrigerator in the kitchen. Could you help me out and run downstairs and get it for me?"

"Sure," Todd said almost leaping out of the room, enjoying the chance to be of some service.

I waited until I heard his footsteps go all the way into the basement before I turned to the group.

"Please listen to me," I said quietly. "I've only got a few seconds to tell you something important that happened last week at the end of Bible study when we were doing our hugs." Quickly and quietly I told them what I had noticed, how I'd felt and how I intended to make sure Todd got hugged this morning, whether or not any of them also chose to hug him. Then I heard Todd's footsteps again and finished quietly by telling the group to think and pray about what I'd said.

Todd returned with the milk and I thanked him for helping out. He smiled broadly and sat down as we continued with the Bible study. Once finished we stood and held hands as we prayed.

We finished with the Lord's Prayer when I once again mentioned the "hug quota" and again explained why we did it. I didn't want to be too obvious and immediately hug Todd, so I decided to hug one or two other people first, but I was going to be sure to hug Todd before he had a chance to leave. When I turned to hug him, I realized that I would have to wait my turn.

The youth were hugging one another, like last week, yet with one crucial difference. This morning they weren't just hugging the kids they liked; they were hugging the kids they loved. Todd's face was shining with the glory of being loved as one kid after another would include him in the large bear hugs. It was as if they'd each silently decide that they would really BE the body of Christ for one another and make that love real this morning. Our hugging took quite a bit longer that morning to finish than it had the week before.

Some of the kids had to hurry to run to school to avoid being late for class. Todd didn't walk the block to school that morning. He didn't run either. I saw him leave and I'll swear that all the way over to the school he floated three feet above the ground.

Jim is the newly hired Campus Pastor at Bemidji State University in Bemidji, Minnesota.

The Crash

As told by Deb Jevne

Immediately after graduating from high school Trevor, Deb Jevne's son, and some of his buddies decided they wanted to see the world, so they left their hometown of West Fargo, North Dakota, for the distant state of Washington. After living there awhile he and his friends decided that this was a little too far away from home so they moved to the Twin Cities in August 1996. Trevor decided to come home that November and spend the Thanksgiving holiday with his family.

Trevor came home late Wednesday night and spent a great Thanksgiving Day with family. That night he and his mother, Deb, decided to get up early on Friday and battle the thousands of "Day after Thanksgiving" shoppers.

"We got up early, went shopping and got acquainted again and had a wonderful time," Deb said. "I kept thinking what a wonderful day this is. I'm going to remember it forever."

That evening Trevor decided that he wanted to hook up with some of his high school buddies, so he took the family car and headed out. He returned home several times unable to find them, got on the phone and tried to call them, and then left again to look for them. He left at 10:30 for the last time.

By 11:20 Trevor hadn't returned, so Deb went to bed thinking that he must have found his friends. At 11:25 Deb's husband, Trent, came into the bedroom.

"Honey, get out of bed. Trevor's been in a serious accident," he said.

Deb's immediate response was that this was some kind of a sick joke, but she soon realized he was serious so she jumped out of bed, got dressed and headed out the door.

During the three-block drive to the scene of the accident Trent told Deb that one of Trevor's friends had come to the house and told him that he had been following Trevor. They had decided to head back home and drop off the car and his friend was going to pick him up and they would head off.

Trevor, heading northbound, had just gone through an intersection when a speeding car came flying into the intersection heading east. At the same time a pickup was crossing the intersection heading south.

"They hit the little truck enough to veer them off to hit the back seat of our car," Deb said. "The police estimate the vehicle was traveling 90 miles per hour in a 25 mile per hour zone."

The force of impact spun the car 360 degrees and sent it sailing into a snow bank. Fortunately Trevor had been wearing his seatbelt otherwise he probably would have been ejected from the car. Despite the seatbelt his head hit the windshield.

"When we got to the scene of the crash he was tucked under the front dash," she said, explaining how odd this was considering he is over six feet tall.

As they approached the accident scene they could see all kinds of emergency lights flashing.

Deb instantly walked up to the car and attempted to talk to Trevor who was just lying there.

"His eyes were wide open, but you could see there was no life behind them," she said. "He didn't blink. He didn't move."

The EMT people were trying to stabilize him. At that time they didn't know if he'd broken his back or neck or if he had any internal bleeding. It took between 35 to 40 minutes to get him out of the car and onto the body-board.

The force of the crash shattered all of the windows in the vehicle that hit Trevor and momentum had carried the car an entire block away from the scene of the accident. The driver and his two passengers only suffered minor cuts and were treated and released that same night.

Trevor was then rushed to the emergency room.

After sitting in the small family emergency waiting room for thirty minutes, Deb decided to go out and see how her son was doing.

"I started walking through the emergency room to see if I could find him," she said. She noticed that the first room was empty but the next one was full of medical staff. As she walked by she thought "Gee, whoever's in there sure must be sick."

She continued to look, but she couldn't find him. She finally asked a nurse if she knew where her son was.

The nurse asked, "Whose your son?"

"Trevor."

She got a funny look on her face and said "Just a minute."

She then stopped a doctor who had been walking by and she explained that it was Trevor's mother.

"I don't have time to talk to her," he said as he headed off into room two.

The nurse then told her she would have to go back to the waiting room because Trevor was in room two.

As the doctor opened the door she could hear a gurgling, gasping noise coming from the room. Later she found out they had been attempting to put a tube down his throat because he was seizing.

The doctor's eventually came in and told the family that he had hit the windshield and they were unsure how much brain damage he had suffered. They also said they had no idea how long it would be before he would come out of his coma, but they did say the tests showed no internal bleeding and no broken bones.

He spent the next week in the intensive care unit hooked up to various machines and tubes.

During the third morning in the hospital Deb, Trent, and Trevor's grandfather were sitting in the room with him. Deb sat next to his still comatose body as she brushed his hair.

"Come on Trevor, wake up."

All of a sudden he opened his eyes, looked at Deb and despite the tube down his throat he managed to blurt out "Mom."

"I thought this was a good sign," she said. "He knew who I was."

Finally the tubes came out and they had to discover if he could do all the little things that most people take for granted. They had to see if he knew how to eat or even go to the bathroom by himself.

After a week he was moved to the rehabilitation unit where he went through occupational, physical and speech therapy. Initially he couldn't hold his head up, he had no coordination of any kind and lights bothered his eyes.

"Head injury patients often act like an older person that has had a stroke," she said. "We went through two and a half months of therapy with him."

Initially he didn't know the difference between a washer and a dryer, and he didn't even know how to get on a bus.

"One of the biggest things that scared him was the mall," she explained. "They brought him there for occupational therapy and he cried the whole time he was there. The light, the sound, the noise and the people were too much for him to comprehend."

Also, anytime he traveled in a car he had to sit in the back seat because he was scared to death of the front seat.

Despite this fear he doesn't remember the accident.

"He lost all memory of the week before the accident and the two weeks after," she explained.

He also has short-term memory loss. He can't even remember the day, which meant so much to his mother, which he had spent shopping with her.

Trevor has been left permanently partially disabled and lives in constant pain. His total hospital bill was in excess of $46,000, and when he is taking his medication, to help him deal with the pain, it will cost anywhere from $500 to $700 a month.

"When his headaches get so bad, he has to inject himself to be able to go to sleep," she said adding that "this isn't easy for someone that is as scared to death of needles as he is."

Many things can set off these vicious headaches. He has to try to maintain an even emotional keel. Extreme emotional highs or lows can set off the pain. He must also carefully monitor his diet since additives like caffeine can give him a headache the following day.

Eventually he was able to go back to work stocking shelves for a former employee. He started out working for one hour in the middle of the night so that there wouldn't be many people around. The less distractions the better. He eventually worked his stamina up to six-hour shifts.

After that Deb decided that she had to do something to stop alcohol impaired drivers from hitting the roads.

Through all of this, Mother's Against Drunk Drivers (MADD) never contacted Deb and she wondered why not. She decided to contact the organization herself to see what could be done, and she found out there was no MADD chapter in the state of North Dakota.

There had been a movement to set up a chapter in the state, but not many people were stepping up to take on the responsibility.

A woman from the Traffic Safety Task Force in Cass County asked Deb if she would speak at a Victims Impact Panel meeting. This is a program in which alcohol offenders are required to attend meetings, as part of their sentence, where victims are given the chance to tell their story.

This woman not only talked Deb into speaking at the Victim's Impact Panel, but she also encouraged her to get involved with MADD. In June 1999 the MADD Cass County Chapter was created and Deb was named the president.

Most of her initial energies were spent on public relations.

"We want to show people we're here," she said. This public relations includes attending "National Night Out", police picnics, police motorcades and being involved in the "Tie One On For Safety" project which involves handing out red ribbons for people to wear to display their support for MADD.

Another service MADD provides is a victim advocate. This volunteer will contact the victims and their families to see if they need any assistance. They can also send out information on how to cope with issues ranging from dealing with injuries to dealing with the court systems.

During her time with MADD, Deb has discovered several common misconceptions people hold about the organization. Some think it is a prohibitionist group.

"That is not the case," she said. "We don't care if you drink. We just don't want you driving after you have been drinking."

Another misconception is that members of MADD sit outside the bars and call the police once they see someone leaving the parking lot.

"We just want people to act like adults and know right from wrong," she said.

Since the accident, things have somewhat returned to normal for Trevor. Looking at him one would never know that he had suffered a terrible accident, but those close to him know he still suffers from that terrible event.

One noticeable thing is that his personality changed. After the crash he has suffered from fits of anger. One minute he'll be fine and the next minute he'll act out like a young child.

"He can blow a gasket," she said, "and say things that Trevor wouldn't normally say." He also still suffers from headaches that are much worse than migraines.

Trevor has often made the comment that he is "sick and tired of being sick and tired."

This accident was definitely a defining moment for Deb. Since that night she worries about both of her sons on the road.

"Being in the car and being aware of it," she said, "you're always watching the other drivers." She cited that studies have shown that three out of every ten drivers are drug or alcohol impaired. "When you are driving you don't know which the three out of ten are. Some may have a little control while others may have none."

Although many state have a legal limits of .10 blood alcohol level it has been proven that people become affected at .05. There has even been a national movement to lower the legal limits to .08.

Another major change in Deb's life has been the large amount of time she has spent with MADD trying to get the word out.

"I'm not about to stop anytime soon," she said. "It's easy to keep going especially when you think back on Trevor in the coma, or going through all of the rehab, and all of the medicine. All of this when the kid that hit him walked away."

It's easy for her to keep pushing forward. All she has to do is think of how poor choices made by an alcohol-impaired driver have drastically changed the life of her son.

The Complete Turnaround

As told by Bethany and Helen Heen

When Bethany Heen began her freshman year at Grand Forks Central High School she was anything but motivated to do well in school. It wasn't uncommon for her to skip classes or to hang out with the "wrong" crowd, and doing her homework was completely out of the question.

"I didn't really feel the need to put in the effort," she explained.

Whether for one period or for an entire day Bethany was missing school at least once a week, if not more. The transition from junior high to senior high was too tempting for her. The open campus policy was too much freedom for her to handle responsibly.

She smoked cigarettes, drank alcohol and did a lot of partying during this year.

"She also did a lot of crawling out her basement bedroom window," Bethany's mother Helen said.

"I even got caught sneaking out a couple of times," Bethany said.

Helen and Bethany's father, Earl, tried yelling at her and even grounding her to get her to change.

"I think one of the things that bothered her was that I didn't want to go to her school conferences in eighth and ninth grade," Helen explained, "I knew she wasn't studying and she was skipping school so I just didn't want to go and hear about it. I felt like I was in the principal's office getting yelled at."

Helen told her daughter that when she went to all of her classes and did all of her homework then she would once again attend her conferences.

"I wasn't asking her to be an A honor roll student," Helen said. "I was just asking her to be an average student, which I knew she was capable of."

The winter of 1996-97 was one of the worst ones in recorded history. It supplied many blizzards and record snowfalls throughout the upper Midwest. When all of the snowfall began to melt in the spring many cities bordering rivers were left devastated by flooding. The Red River was especially destructive in Grand Forks that year, and it disrupted the lives of thousands of people.

When Grand Forks was overtaken by floodwaters her high school had to close because of flooding. The Heen's basement was also completely flooded out, leaving Bethany without a bedroom. Her parents thought it would be good for her to attend school in Helen's hometown of Pelican Rapids, Minnesota. After a week, she went to live in Pelican Rapids for the next six weeks.

"I thought that getting as much school as she could would help make a difference for her," Helen said.

Despite transferring to Pelican Rapids and finishing out the school year, she was given straight D's in all of her classes that she had been failing before the flood. She received D's in all five of the classes she took that semester.

Although none of her coursework in Pelican Rapids counted toward her grades, Bethany was quick to praise the experience.

"I liked it there," she said. "It was a good experience."

"I would have to say that I noticed even a little more wildness in her after the flood," Helen said. "We had a FEMA trailer in back of the house for her to stay in and it got to be a regular party house out there." They eventually had to get rid of the trailer.

All of the sudden something just clicked inside of Bethany. Things got to the point where she finally admitted her ways of operating had to change.

"Life goes really fast," she said adding that she didn't want it to pass her by.

"I wanted to make something of myself," she said knowing she was headed down the wrong path if she didn't change.

"People can't make you change. You can only change yourself," Bethany said, "You have to have your own mind and you can't do what other people say. You have to be your own person. If you don't do what you believe and you just follow everyone else then you're going to become a victim and you won't go anywhere."

Bethany transformed from follower to leader. Helen explained that she went from being worried about having a "best" friend to having many friends.

When Bethany first announced that she was going to change her ways, Helen hoped that she was sincere, but with her past record it was more than easy to be a little skeptical.

"During the summer she kept saying, 'You just watch...You just watch...I'm going to change'..." Helen said. "I told her I had to see it to believe it."

"I love to prove people wrong," Bethany said.

Helen knew Bethany was capable of making the change, but she needed to see more than just words before believing the changes were for real.

"The first proof I had was when I found out that she had no absences during the first month of her sophomore year," Helen said.

Even her teachers, who remembered what she'd been like her freshman year, wanted to see the proof that she had really changed.

A couple of weeks into her sophomore year Bethany came home upset with some of her teachers. "They're not treating me like I'm going to change," she told her mother.

"Beth, you're going to have to earn that," Helen told her, aware that it was going to take some time before the "new" Bethany would be totally accepted.

During that time she also leaned heavily on the support of two Central High School educators, Mr. Kasowski and Mrs. Molenaar.

Once Bethany made her change public, many of her friends quit calling. Some of them asked her what was wrong with her, but many of them were proud of her and her new successes. Some were even a little jealous.

"I still talked to the people, but we didn't do anything together anymore," Bethany explained, "I picked a new crowd that made better choices."

Bethany did prove that she was capable of making the needed changes. During her tenth grade year she earned a place on the A honor roll four times.

After this turnaround Helen kept her promise and once again began attending conferences. "They were fun then," she said with a smile.

It was her junior year before many of her teachers realized that she meant business. After that many of her teachers and principals were extremely proud of the changes she had made, especially those that had taught her in eighth or ninth grade.

During the beginning of her junior year, Bethany took on two paper routes on the other end of town. She would get up at five in the morning, drive for fifteen minutes, spend an hour delivering the papers, and then drive back home. She did this for a year and a half without ever once calling in sick. She then got another route closer to home, which she held for another eight months.

Her change in lifestyle included quitting smoking and adding the game of pocket billiards to her life. She spent many weekend evenings shooting pool at Lucky's Pool Hall while her friends were busy partying. She eventually joined a league.

During her senior year she delivered papers, worked for a local restaurant and babysat up to three times a week for a family with five children (ages 7, 6, 5, 3, and 2). All this while she maintained her near perfect grade point average.

"I had been trying to gain attention by being a bad girl," Bethany explained. "When I started being good I noticed that I got a lot more attention. The principal would stop me in the hall and tell me that everyone was really proud of me. It made me feel really good. I just wanted to keep it up."

Bethany was also one of the 40 students nominated as recipient of the Personal Best Awards. During the recognition awards evening, the principal came over to congratulate Helen and Earl on how well their daughter was doing.

"I didn't feel like I was in the principal's office anymore," Helen said.

The possibilities of where Bethany would be if she hadn't changed her ways are unlimited.

"I possibly could have been a dropout, possibly pregnant, and if I hadn't dropped out I would have had a D average," she said. "Being bad gets old. Continuously trying to find a cover up so you don't get detention gets old."

She also encourages other youth that have adopted the "School sucks" mentality to get over it and think positive about it.

Despite Bethany's miraculous turnaround she suffered a setback as she attempted to enroll in her hometown University of North Dakota (UND). She was missing a core curriculum algebra class, which she had avoided with the desire to get a perfect 4.0 grade point average her last semester of high school.

Since she was short this class a great deal of weight was placed on her ACT test scores. She scored a 15 on the test. She needed to get a 17.

Bethany's application and subsequent appeal to the University was denied despite having glowing recommendations from both Grand Forks Central High School administration and teachers.

Although losing the final appeal was devastating for Bethany, she felt that it must have happened for a reason.

"Even though we may not understand why things happen, they do for a reason," she said. "It's fate."

She has since decided to attend Northwest Technical College in East Grand Forks, Minnesota. After taking general courses she plans to enroll at UND. Her eventual goal is to attend law school and possibly become a defense attorney.

"I think that when I do get in," she said, "I'm going to impress their pants off."

Bethany earlier said that she loves to prove people wrong. She feels the University was wrong when it didn't allow her to attend, and she is going to do everything within her power to prove she belongs. This is just another stepping stone for Bethany.

She operates under a very famous motto: "What doesn't kill me makes me stronger."

The Break

As told by Craig Richie

Many times we don't realize how important life's defining moments are when they happen. There was one event in my life that I didn't gain a greater appreciation for until much later in life.

I was twenty years old, just finishing my sophomore year in college at Adrian College in Michigan. I had wanted to go to law school since I was a sixth grader and in order to do so I needed to maintain at least a B average. I wasn't a great student, but I worked really hard to maintain the B average.

My first year I got all B's. I couldn't seem to get any A's, but I also didn't get any C's. I worked hard and found a way to get B's.

During the first semester of my sophomore year I got the same. During the second semester I was going to school and playing on the baseball team. There was a fellow on campus named Howard Emmerich, but everyone called him "Doc." He was a doctor of divinity and campus chaplain.

Doc was in his mid-fifties. He had played halfback on the Geneva College (Pennsylvania) football team back in the era when Geneva played the powerhouse teams like Harvard. He played racquetball every Saturday with the college president way before the days of everyone working out.

I didn't know him as well as some of the guys did, but I was taking a religion of the world course from him during this particular semester.

In addition to his course, I was also taking courses in sociology and literature and doing well in both of these courses. If I were to get an A on the course finals I would earn an A in the class for the semester. If I received a B on the final then I would earn a B for the semester grades. I was right on the border.

I studied hard for the finals, but I flunked both of them. I can't tell you what happened on the one, but on the literature one the professor only tested on the last day of class. I was there that day, but I was tired and didn't study the information from the last day of class. Regardless of the reasons, I still flunked both finals.

Because of these failures I got C's in both classes and thought I would never be able to get to law school. In order to maintain my B average I would now have to get two A's to balance out my grade point average, and I had never gotten an A before. I was down six credit hours.

I remember lying in bed with my face against the wall in the fetal position. I can still visualize the cement block wall that I had stared at in my agony.

Later I went to talk to the sociology and literature professors and tried to explain my dilemma. Neither of them was willing to change the grades.

In desperation I went to Doc to tell him what my problem was. I explained how I wanted to go to law school and how this could prevent me from being able to get in. I had a solid B (85%) in Doc's class. I told Doc what my grade was and he told me to come back and see him tomorrow.

The next day I came back to see him wearing my high school letter jacket. I can still see the face of this bald, virile man that wore glasses. He looked right at me and poked me right on the letter of my letterman's jacket.

"That means something to me," he said, "I'm going to give you that A."

Whenever I tell this story I still get tears in my eyes. I have trouble fighting back crying. Some people might say that he was doing this for all of the wrong reasons or that he was giving a jock a break, but he was really saying that I meant something. He was telling me that I had some worth.

He knew that I had been working hard, and this was his way of telling me that I was significant and that I could do it. I went home that summer knowing that I could indeed make it, and from that point on I knew I was going to make it into law school. All I had to do was earn another A and the B average would be maintained.

I didn't deserve the break that Doc had given me. This was his way of showing me God's salvation, which is a wonderful thing that was given to all of us. There is no way it could be earned, it is simply a gift. He wasn't telling me what it was to be a Christian, instead he was showing me.

Had Doc not given me a break like this I more than likely would have lost all hope and probably never made it to law school. Doc's display of grace empowered me to move forward. He showed me that I was worth something.

He taught me that it is my responsibility to help others up the ladder instead of standing above them putting my foot on their heads as they try to fight their way up the rungs.

Doc cared about everybody on campus. He was so well loved on campus that one kid had a picture of Doc on his dorm room wall. He literally loved the guy.

I never really got a chance to tell Doc how much he helped me out. I didn't realize what a big part he had played in my life until my son went to college and they didn't help him out. He eventually lost all hope, got discouraged and dropped out. He quit school because he didn't think he could do it anymore. There was nobody willing to help him out.

This school had lost its vision of helping kids out and was more concerned with keeping its doors open. There's a real danger with this.

We are all responsible for being like Doc. I'm sure there are times when we might get conned, but I'd much rather be conned than have no feeling at all.

I guess I'd just like to thank Doc Emmerich for all the doors his simple act of kindness opened for me.

Craig is an attorney in Fargo, North Dakota and a huge advocate for youth sports.

Bottom of the Ninth

As told by Bucky Burgau

It was the 1969 Minnesota Class B State Amateur Baseball Tournament. It was the bottom of the ninth and Perham was leading Browntown 5-4. Browntown had runners on second and third and two outs.

Perham's fourteen-year-old second baseman, Bucky Burgau, had grown up around baseball. That summer he played on Perham's Babe Ruth and American Legion teams in addition to the town's amateur team.

Bucky stood ready as the two-out pitch was delivered. Immediately after the bat hit the ball it began rolling toward him. He scooped up the ground ball, turned toward first base and threw it to his father who was waiting for the ball. The game was over.

He and his father had recorded the final out together.

As players ran on the field to celebrate, Bucky remembers that he reached his father first.

"Dad was the first one I reached to hug," he told.

This state title was extremely exciting for the Perham team. They had been on the threshold of winning the title many times before, but had never quite been able to get over the hump. This team consisted of a variety of players including five players still in high school and several older men offering leadership.

There are probably a million different stories that could be told about Perham's run through the single elimination tournament, but one of the most touching would have to be the story of young Bucky and his father.

Earlier that year Bucky's parents had gotten divorced and his father moved away to Gwinner, North Dakota. His dad continued to manage Perham's amateur team and drove back every Wednesday night for games.

As one could imagine times were tough for Bucky. He was bitter about everything that happened and held many hard feelings.

"Playing baseball rejuvenated good feelings with Dad," he explained. "At the time I didn't think much of the father-son thing, but as the years went by it became more and more meaningful."

Following the championship season Bucky was able to play two more years with his father. With years to reflect he has realized just how meaningful this time really was.

Tossing the final out to his father was definitely a defining moment for Bucky.

"From that point on I knew that I wanted to be involved in coaching and education," he said. Bucky went on to coach the Moorhead American Legion baseball team for 27 years (winning 883 games), Concordia College's baseball team for 22 years (winning 425 games) and he recently became an assistant coach the Northern League Fargo-Moorhead Redhawks.

Despite being a winning coach Bucky gladly accepted the mentoring role that accompanies coaching. He took this as serious as he did his on-the-field strategies.

"The importance of the father figure is more important than wins and losses," he said.

Bucky always had a special place in his heart for children of divorced parents. It always tore him up to see players whose parents were divorced, and the father who never took the time to come and see his son play.

If one of Bucky's players didn't have a father at home he would take special effort to be supportive of him.

"If they did something good or something traumatic happened in their life I would either call them or take them out for lunch," he said. "I knew what it was like not to have a dad at home."

Bucky credited several of his former coaches for rallying around him and showing him a special interest.

"Their support was much more important to me than the sports," he said. "These coaches showed me that you need good folks to help you along the way."

Bucky also knows how influential a coach can be to his athletes. Thirty years after the fact he still remembers an incident that happened on the field. After hitting his first home run in amateur ball the entire team came out to shake his hand except his father.

"He probably expected it from me," Bucky said, "but he never said anything to me."

This taught Bucky what a profound effect a coach can have on the lives of his players. He knows the importance of a simple pat on the back or a word of praise.

"Who knows? They may take something we say or do with them for the next thirty years," he said. "Obviously I did."

Bucky's father, who now lives in Montana, knows how important the time spent on the baseball field was to his son. Bucky made sure he told him. They still get the chance to spend quality time together as they meet for hunting trips every year.

Often many of us don't take the time to let others know how special they are to us. There probably wasn't a father or son alive that didn't get a lump in his throat the first time he watched the movie "Field of Dreams" when Kevin Costner's character was given the chance to play catch with his deceased father.

Many times it's the simple things that mean the most. A game of catch, a walk in the park or a day fishing on the lake can mean so much. It's not what you're doing that's important, it's that you're doing it together with someone you love.

Bucky is currently the coach of the Concordia Cobber's Baseball Team during each spring season and is an assistant coach with the Northern League Redhawks.

The Decision That Weighed on My Mind
By
Dean Cota

My friend asked me to write a little story about how I changed my life. He wanted me to talk about the defining moments that led me to drastically change my life. I have often wanted to share my story and was given the opportunity to do so on the local evening news. I jumped at the chance to tell you what I did and how it has transformed my life. Some things may seem trivial, but I ask you to step into my shoes and my frame of mind during the story. So here goes, a professional writer I am not, but an interesting story I do believe.

Deep-fried bread, ice cream with hot fudge, potatoes and steak, and Mom's fried chicken.

WOW! I loved those foods. I could eat them everyday until I was so full that I would get sick. For years I ate these types of food until I made the decision to change. That decision didn't happen until I weighed 548 pounds.

By the age of 32 I had grown to the weight of 532 pounds, a weight that probably would have killed me if it continued to increase.

I was always a heavy person. As a sixth grader I weighed 315 pounds, and I left high school weighing in at 415 pounds. Over the years I was able to maintain this weight and actually lost some when I began working for the Fargo-Moorhead Family YMCA.

While working there I could exercise and play basketball whenever I wanted and eventually dropped down to 380. I didn't feel my problem was all that bad. As long as I worked out I could eat whatever I wanted and still lose weight.

I left the YMCA after six years and in less than a year I gained 100 pounds.

Why? Because I ate as much as I did before, but I was no longer able to work out. My weight slowly rose from there.

How did my weight ever get so out of control? I often contemplated that question when I was feeling depressed. Although I hid it well, depression started to play a large factor in my life the heavier I got. As I thought about it all, I looked back on my childhood.

I don't blame my mother and father in the least. They were raised in the age of providing well for your family. We never went hungry and we often splurged. I could sit at the table as long as I felt I was still hungry. Nobody twisted my arm or lifted the fork to my mouth. No one called the pizza man after I left home for college.

Nobody was to blame other than myself. I ate because I loved to eat. I loved food. When I went to college, it was just natural to order pizza or eat at a buffet to get the most for my money.

I always hated being fat, but I had lots of friends who treated me well. I didn't let the obesity bring me too far down at that time.

At one point in my life I had contemplated gastric bypass surgery (more commonly known as stomach stapling). I had gone in for an emergency appendectomy in 1992 and the healing process took much longer than normal. Fat tissue that surrounded my muscle didn't allow the incision to properly heal.

During an appointment my doctor asked how much I would pay for a good car. I told him that if I knew it would last I would pay up to $4000-$5000. He then asked me how much I would pay to extend my life by five to ten years. He proceeded to tell me about gastric bypass surgery and put me in touch with doctors that performed the procedure.

I thought about it for a long time and at that time my insurance covered the operation. So I started the process but was scared away from doing it after hearing some of the experiences surgical patients had.

I went on living my life. Over the next five years I had two surgeries for an incisional hernia, both caused by improper healing from the first surgery's incision. These surgeries coupled with my mindset got me to once again start thinking about having the gastric bypass surgery.

Now let me tell you a little about that mindset. I know that many people face a weight problem and most of them are perfectly content with who they are and how God made them. I, however, was not happy at all.

I had grown up a popular kid in high school playing sports, being elected student body president, sang in the choir and did a variety of other things to keep active. I maintained a lot of friendships, but there was always something missing. Throughout college I had many friends, that has never been a problem for me, but still there was always something missing.

During all these years I faced a lot of verbal abuse from people who didn't even know me. I wasn't always able to do things that my friends could because of my size. I never went swimming without a T-shirt because of the way I looked. I was always the last guy to take a shower after gym because so many of the upper classmen would tease and make all those fat jokes.

I quit the basketball team for two reasons. First, because the uniforms were always too small and secondly because a coach told me in ninth grade that even though I was a decent player I wouldn't play much because I was too slow.

Throughout the years it got worse, especially once I left employment with the YMCA and gained more weight. It not only started to affect my mentality, but it also started to affect many of the friendships I had. I also believe at this time that depression started to fall into the mix.

I hid it well at work and with a few friends, but nobody understands what I felt when I went home and closed my door.

I didn't like to go to movies because I couldn't sit in the seat. I didn't like to go out in public much because of the stares and comments from perfect strangers. It got even worse when I would go to friend's houses and they would ask me to sit in certain chairs. I understood, but nonetheless it hurt.

All these things started to drive me into a little shell. I would go home after work with my chips and dip and eat them, and later I would order a pizza. For many smoking is a crutch, for some drinking, but for myself it was food.

If I was eating I was happy. Nothing could bother me. I was alone in my home enjoying what I enjoyed doing the most. It gets bad when you call the pizza place and they know exactly who you are and where you live and what you want to order. But you know, when I was all done eating, there I was, still alone, depressed that I had no one to do anything with.

You see, that was another thought that kept running through my head. Who would be attracted to me, who would want to spend time with a person as fat as I was? I didn't believe that anyone would want to do that.

It drove me further into such a lonely feeling. I felt that I would be alone and remain large for the rest of my life.

Another problem facing large individuals is clothing. Where do you purchase a size 66 pair of jeans? Not at Wal-Mart or Big K, I can guarantee you that. Most big and tall stores don't even have them in that size.

Special mail order is where you had to go. What a treat that is. Pay more, take a chance you're gonna order the right size and hope it looks as good as it did in the picture.

Often you get it and it's the wrong size or you just don't like it. Then you have to send it back which causes more cost and delays. It just gets to be such a problem that you get by on very little clothing.

I look back on my childhood and remember chasing down kids in junior high because of some of the things they said. Everyone thought I was slow, but I did all right for a big guy back then. I played the role of the big bully. Why shouldn't I? If they wanted to say some of the things they did, then I was gonna use my size to my advantage. Once I caught them, they would pay and they never told because of what might happen next time. It's funny once you show them what you're made of how differently they treat you from that point on.

Throughout my life I was ashamed of how I looked. What people thought of me constantly drove me crazy. I would see someone look at me funny and start to imagine all kinds of cruel things that people were saying about me. As time progressed I also felt my self-confidence starting to fade away. I felt I was a good person, but my weight was affecting many aspects of my life.

I loved to coach kids, but I didn't feel I was always giving them the best experience. I felt I was a good and valuable employee to the company I worked for, but the heavier I got the harder it was for me to do my job. Going to work in specially made sports pants bothered me because I didn't feel I was carrying the type of look needed at the professional level.

So what did I do? First I asked God to lead me in the right direction. Obviously I couldn't conquer this problem on my own.

In the fall of 1997 I had an emergency surgery for one of my incisional hernias. At this time the doctor was very persistent in suggesting that I have the gastric bypass surgery. He was persistent enough for me to reconsider having the surgery.

I am thankful to him for putting this thought into my head. I believed that it was time to tackle this problem, for if I didn't I was unsure where I'd end up. I experienced some very bad thoughts throughout the year leading up to this surgery.

I was very lonely and very disappointed in myself because I couldn't conquer this problem. I had, believe it or not, contemplated suicide on a number of occasions. I thank the Lord that it was only contemplation and that I never carried through with anything.

It would have been so easy to take a trip home to my parents farm and go out for a little walk in the woods with one of the rifles and end it all, but something kept telling me that wasn't the right thing to do.

I was in very bad shape when I was alone. When I was out and about nobody could tell anything was wrong.

I informed my supervisors at work that I needed to have this surgery. In order to have the surgery though, I needed to do a three month diet plan with a registered dietician with weekly weigh-ins and monthly meetings. I began the process and figured that in January of 1998 I would be able to have the surgery and my work agreed to give me the needed time off.

Everything was going very well. I had lost 48 pounds in three months simply by giving up pop and chips. I was preparing for the time when surgery would come. The doctors wrote letters of recommendation and took pictures in order to make the decision to cover the surgery easier for our insurance company. Then it happened, I received a phone call from our controller at work who worked with our insurance program.

The surgery wasn't covered under the existing policy. It had been covered under a prior plan, but when we switched policies it no longer was.

I was devastated. I was not sure what to think. The surgery date was cancelled.

Once again negative thoughts started running through my head. I believed I would be this way for the rest of my life. I wasn't sure if I could handle it and I slipped back into my old thought patterns.

In the next month I regained all but 16 of the 48 pounds I had lost. I continued to binge and also started to drink more at this time. This was how I got away from everything.

If I was out eating and drinking with friends I was not at home sitting alone thinking of all of this. Once again the good Lord smiled down upon me and answered prayers from my family and me. The controller at my business started talking with the insurance company to change our plan and get the surgery covered under our policy.

This lady was a blessing from above. Throughout the next two months she had many meetings with the insurance company. I even attended one of those meetings to give my side of the story. She worked very hard to get this change and gave me a call in January 1998 to say that the plan would be changed and the insurance would cover the surgery. Once again I was elated.

Talk about a roller coaster of emotions over a short period of time. At times it was very heart wrenching but I now know that sometimes we need to face hardship in order to realize the good doings of the people that surround us.

On February 5, 1998, I entered the hospital to have the surgery. I finally knew it was going to happen. It was one of the single-most positive days of my life. On this day I was being offered the opportunity, with the help of so many people, to change my life.

It started with the doctors being persistent and putting the thought in my head. The people at my place of business fought to get it covered through our insurance and also gave me the time off to have it done. My family was also there to support me every step of the way. Three of my sisters, Irene, Norma, and Lois went to extreme lengths to offer assistance and a place to stay throughout my recovery.

Norma traveled from Colorado with her two children and stayed with me throughout the recovery after my gastric bypass surgery. I am forever grateful for the incredible sacrifices made by all three of my sisters and to all the many friends who supported me through it all.

I couldn't eat for the four days following the surgery, and if all went well I would be able to go home five days after the surgery. Each day I got better and things looked good.

I was very excited to go home and continue the recovery, but then things took another turn for the worse on the evening before I was supposed to be released.

I experienced some of worst pain I had ever experienced in my life. I could hardly breath without severe pain shooting throughout my sides. They called in a doctor in the middle of the night and brought a portable x-ray machine to my room to do testing.

The next morning I was taken for special testing. They found that I had blood clots in my lungs, something I later learned could be fatal, but they caught it soon enough and corrected it with medication. This meant an extended stay in the hospital until the blood clots broke up and the doctors were certain I would be healthy enough to go home.

I spent the next six weeks recovering with the help of my sister from Colorado.

The first three weeks consisted of eating nothing but soft food and liquids. About a half cup at a time seven times per day.

Wow what a change! Going from chips and dips to a little bit of food here and there.

It didn't matter. I wasn't hungry and I wanted this change so bad that it didn't even enter my mind how little I was eating. My sister made certain that I followed the plan exactly how it was written. I believe this was the start to establishing my new thought and eating patterns.

The weight loss started happening for me quite rapidly. I attended a nephew's wedding about three months after surgery and had already lost 70 pounds. My family was amazed.

For the first time in years I stepped on a dance floor and danced with my sisters. I always loved to dance but was too self-conscious to do so. This was truly the start of a new life.

In the spring of 1999 I had another surgery to remove some of the excess skin that had remained from the rapid weight loss. This surgery was what they called a tummy tuck. They removed a 7-inch wide by 54-inch long piece of skin and fat from my midsection. I know it sounds bad but it took off about forty pounds alone. Now I don't have a big stomach hanging over my belt-line.

That was the last surgery for now, but I am considering one more to take off some excess on my legs and to tighten up other areas.

I now weigh about 265 pounds. I walk tall and stand proud. I'm not just proud of how I look, but how I've taken this problem head on and conquered it.

During the Fourth of July I went home to our All-City Reunion. I had not seen some of my classmates or friends for over ten years and many did not even recognize me. They had to do a double take to make sure it was me.

Yes, life has changed considerably for me. I enjoy going out in public and doing just about anything. All the looks and comments I have received leave me speechless.

Not only am I healthier physically, but mentally. I no longer worry about what people think. I also know that I can take on a challenge, follow it through, and be successful. Life is a wonderful thing, some choose to live in pain, I chose to make a change.

What a beautiful outcome!

(Anyone interested in talking with Dean about his experiences should contact him at cotakid@yahoo.com)

The World is a Little Less Beautiful Today
By
Chad A. Filley

Have you ever met someone that you instantly knew was special? Even though you may have only known this person for a short time they were able to make a lasting impact on you.

It might have been a simple piece of advice they offered or it may have involved extending some truly needed help. I have seen people that barely know one another discussing personal issues that they wouldn't think of sharing with their family and friends.

These interactions can involve pointing out that someone possesses a special gift that they are totally unaware of. This was the entire basis of the "Wizard of Oz." It finally took the wizard to announce to each character that they already possessed the very qualities they sought after.

Another one of these encounters might involve a simple act of kindness. I'm not saying that opening the door for someone or letting a car in front of you during rush hour is necessarily going to make a major difference, but you never know when a considerate act might make a lasting impact on someone else.

Although I can think of several people that have truly touched my life by their offerings of unconditional love, I'm going to talk about two separate instances. The first one was a women whose name I don't even know that offered me unquestioned kindness.

In July 1994 I was part of a charter bus caravan heading to a national youth gathering in Atlanta. Our ten-bus caravan, full of youth and chaperones, stopped at a rest stop in Southern Illinois. It isn't hard to imagine that whenever we decided to stop it was going to take at least a half-hour if not more.

For obvious reasons that I'm not going to get into, the males on the trip were able to get in and out of the bathrooms much sooner, so about half the time was spent waiting for the females to have a chance to use the restrooms. At one rest stop the women even commandeered the men's room in order to save travel time.

Being among the first to use the bathroom I had quite a bit of time to waste. It was about 11:30 a.m. and the itinerary had us scheduled for a lunch stop an hour and a half down the road.

As I stood there talking to some of the kids from the bus I noticed an African-American family (mother, father, teenage son and daughter) sitting at a picnic table eating lunch.

I walked up to them and jokingly asked them what was for lunch.

The mother looked up at me and without hesitating said "We're having sandwiches, chips and soda. Sit down and join us."

"No, I was just kidding," I told the women.

"If you're really hungry sit down and join us," she said.

I sat down at the picnic table next to her obviously embarrassed children. I'm sure they couldn't believe their mother would invite some stranger to sit down to eat with them. We introduced ourselves and I sat down to a feast fit for a king.

She opened her cooler and gave me a can of coke, a bag chips and then proceeded to tell me to help myself to the bread and the sandwich meat.

As we broke bread together we talked about ourselves and had a great meal. All this as I waited for the buses to get loaded.

Just as I was about to leave I thanked her for her hospitality and then asked her why she fed me.

Before she could answer her daughter and son shook their heads up and down in unison.

"Mama is always willing to help someone out," the girl said.

"That's right," she said, "You came and asked for food which told me you were hungry. I don't know who you are. For all I know you might be Jesus Christ."

She then added "Remember what the Bible says. Whatever you do for the least of these you do for me."

Although I saw several world class speakers at the national gathering none of them had as powerful a message or as big an impact on me as this women and her family did. Their willingness to share some food and much more importantly some love with me was truly inspiring.

I was also fortunate enough to meet someone that made a huge impact on me when I spent the first week of June at the Roughrider Health Conference at Medora, ND in 1999. That person was Jean Heinert.

My first encounter with Jean was a memorable one. I had just finished eating supper with long-time friend, Darian Schaubert, who was presenting a conference on diabetes. After eating we decided to meet up with some other friends that were relaxing at one of the saloons.

After opening the door to the screened-in patio a short women in her fifties walked up to me demanding a "five dollar cover charge" payment. Noticing that she was wearing a conference badge I grabbed her, put my hand over her mouth and proceeded to make it look as though I was giving her a big kiss.

"I guess that will teach me," she said victoriously raising her fist up into the air as she walked back to her table of friends.

Later that evening we had the chance to talk for a few minutes, and I found out that she was an elementary school counselor from Williston, ND. Our conversation was mostly superficial and included the exchange of jokes and humorous anecdotes. Of course half the fun of these conferences is getting the chance to unwind with new and interesting educators from around the state.

The following afternoon I attended a breakout session that dealt with the issues associated with death and dying. The presentation was given by a female funeral director that was very honest and open in answering questions. During the question/answer session I asked her if funeral directors ever get used to doing funerals for children. The funeral director's open and honest response opened a floodgate of questions from the attendees. It was a great session.

As I was walking out of the room I noticed Jean sitting at one of the tables with her friends from Williston.

"I wanted to tell you that you really have a gift," she said, "You are able to ask tough questions in a caring and concerned manner. Both of the questions you asked were good ones."

I sat down next to Jean to get her take on the session and soon discovered that one of the reasons she had attended this session was that she had been battling cancer for the past eleven years. As she revealed this to me she pulled her swollen feet out from under the table revealing that they were more than twice the normal size.

"I'm really retaining fluids," she told me.

Over the next couple of days I found out that Jean and I had a great deal in common. One major commonality was our past work in youth ministry. Jean had worked for eleven years at St. Joseph's Catholic Church before going to Northern State University to earn her master's degree in counseling. Our conversations became more and more revealing after discovering that we had both been youth ministers.

She told me how she had decided to stop taking chemotherapy to battle the cancer. She had decided to scrap medical treatment and combat the cancer with faith and prayers.

During the final awards banquet Jean's group won an award for being the most inspirational group. It was obvious to anyone that met her that she was someone to be admired.

My wife, Candace, was going to be starting a new job as a home transcriptionist. Part of her new job required going to Williston for two weeks of procedural training. These two weeks were going to be stressful for the family both emotionally and financially. Candy was going to have to stay in a hotel for two weeks which was certainly going to run up quite a bill.

As I left the conference I asked Jean if she was going to be home on Sunday. When she said yes I explained to her that the boys and I were going to be bringing Candy to Williston on Sunday and that I would call her when we arrived.

"Good. I want to meet the three boys that I've heard so much about," she said.

People often say I'll call you or let's get together and they don't really mean it. With Jean things were just different. She was such a good and sincere person that I really did want to call her and introduce my family to her.

After arriving and checking Candy into the hotel room, I called Jean who immediately invited us over to her house. After arriving and meeting her husband we sat down to talk for awhile. Once they found out Candy would be staying in a hotel for two weeks they offered to let her stay at their house.

After talking it over it over for awhile it was agreed upon. Candy would stay that evening at the hotel and then would spend the remaining time at their home. Dick and Jean probably had no idea how much this meant to us financially, but it really helped out a family just struggling to keep its head above water.

During the next two weeks I had plenty of things to keep me busy including watching the boys and going to a job interview, but I was also selfishly a little jealous of Candy getting to spend two weeks with Jean and her husband. She was able to spend evenings getting to know them. She even participated in a prayer group they hosted. Candy was able to experience the beauty and joy of Jean. When the boys and I came to pick her up it was easy to see that Candy had a great experience.

As I mentioned before I had a job interview and was offered a teaching job in Halstad, Minnesota. After deciding to accept the job the rest of the summer was spent getting ready to move. Unfortunately we lost touch with Dick and Jean until after we moved.

Candy wrote a letter to them to let them know our new address and to let them know how things were going at our new house. A short while later we received a letter from Dick telling that Jean had died.

I was standing in front of my second hour sophomore history class when Candy called to tell me the news. I immediately felt terrible. Although I hadn't known her very long I felt like I had lost one of my closest friends.

I instantly thought about the circumstances surrounding the first time we met. I thought about how she and her husband opened their home for Candy to stay. I thought about how the young children at her school must have been heartbroken. I thought about all of the lives she must have touched during her tenure as a youth minister. I thought about how bravely she faced the dreadful disease of cancer head-on. I thought about what a loss her death was to mankind.

I hung up the phone and told my students "I just received the news that a very special friend died." After a short pause I said, "The world is a little less beautiful today."

For the Love of Freedom

As told by Minh Tran

Minh Tran lived in North Vietnam until 1953 when he was forced to move to South Vietnam. He had always treasured his freedom and when the Communists took over in 1953 he and his family fled to the south.

He had been taking classes in English at a local night school before he was forced to leave his home and continued to take classes after arriving in the Southern half of his homeland.

In December 1956 he was hired to work at the United States Embassy in Saigon. He worked for the general service office and was in charge of housing maintenance. He had a staff of more than 100 handymen working for him.

"I made sure all of the offices were in good shape," Minh said, "and I made sure that there was good housing available for the American personnel."

If embassy personnel had a plumbing, electrical or air-conditioning problem, Minh would send someone out to fix it.

In 1966 Minh was drafted into the Vietnamese Army and because of his fluent English was put to work as a translator. He worked with United States Task Force Oregon, part of the Military Intelligence Detachment (MID). This later became part of the reactivated Americal Division.

Minh was put in charge of verbal translations and reading translations of documents.

Despite being part of a war, Minh never had mixed feelings. From the time he had fled North Viet Nam he felt the need to be part of the free world.

"I felt I was doing the right thing at the time," he said. "I still feel the same today."

Minh was in the military up until the end of the war in April 1975. On April 29, 1975, he went to the embassy hoping to evacuate the country. The American embassy had two areas, one on the roof and the other in the courtyard, in which helicopters were landing to airlift people to safety. Minh waited in line on the courtyard.

At one point he was sent from the courtyard into the embassy and told to head up to the roof landing pad. While heading up the stairs he even saw the American ambassador, Graham Martin. Eventually, amidst the confusion, Minh was sent back down to the courtyard.

"It was then that I knew time was running out," he said.

When he arrived back on the ground he could see that the evacuation was stopping.

"I had been very close to getting on one of the helicopters," Minh explained. Earlier he had even given up the chance to get on a helicopter. There were two openings, but he had decided to stay back with a friend of his that was waiting to get on a chopper with his four children.

"I gave up my seat," he said. "I was confident that I could get on the next one."

After coming to the realization that he wasn't going to be evacuated, Minh went home completely dejected and upset.

During the taking of Saigon there was some minor resistance from the South Vietnamese, but for the most part everybody knew the war was over.

Soon afterward the North Vietnamese interrogated all soldiers including Minh. He had burned all records that linked him with either the embassy or the military. Minh was eventually sent to a three-day re-education camp.

"The word police told me that I was wrong and they were right," he said. "They told us we had to follow the rules. They also fed us with a great deal of communist and socialist propaganda. We had no choice other than to follow the rules because we were the losers."

For the next several months he did a variety of odd jobs. For awhile he was in charge of running a small store that sold used fans, electronics and hi-fi equipment. During this entire time he was looking for a way to escape the country.

In January 1977 his brother had found a way to get out of the country near Phen Rang City, 350 miles north of Saigon. For some reason the communist police found out and arrested Minh and the others.

"I believe the local owner of the boat reported us to the police," Minh said. "We were arrested and put into jail."

Although due process was uncommon in Vietnam, he and the others were put on trial and sentenced to eighteen months for illegally trying to flee the country. The trials were held to publicly warn others not to try attempting to escape.

Minh was put into jail on January 20, 1977. The first few months he was put into a 20 by 20 cell that housed over forty men. They were given very little to eat and many of the prisoners were suffering from dysentery and some form of skin rash.

"If we wanted medicine," Minh said, "we had to contact family members and have them bring it to us."

There was even a female prisoner that had a baby while in prison. Once born her child was then considered to be a prisoner too.

"At first I felt like the sky was falling on me. I thought this would be the end of me," Minh said. Eventually he began talking with other prisoners and they were able to lift up one another's spirits.

"We began to gain a strong feeling of determination to survive," he explained. "I soon realized that this wouldn't be the end of me."

After several months Minh was transferred to a larger cell and eventually allowed to work outside in the vegetable fields during the days.

If someone died their body would be moved out in the middle of the night by the guards. This was done so that nobody would become too alarmed.

The guards weren't cruel people, but they did mean business.

"If anyone made a mistake they were put into solitary with handcuffs and shackles," he said.

When Minh was eventually released after fourteen months, he was suffering from malnutrition and had to be treated with acupuncture because he was no longer able to walk.

Surprisingly Minh wasn't happy after his eventual release.

"I felt like I was being released from a small prison to a large prison of communism," he said. "I was now more determined than ever to get out."

After being released Minh went home to Saigon where he was informed that the local police were going to confiscate his home. They told him they were doing this because of his background.

Minh was more determined than ever to get out now.

He had heard that the government had made provisions for ethnic Chinese to get out of the country if they paid the government.

"Nine members of my family and I disguised ourselves as Chinese and arranged a boat trip to get out."

They were never once questioned about leaving because they were able to provide the needed payment of gold. Each person leaving had to provide ten taiels (approximately twelve ounces) of gold to the police.

Minh didn't have to pay because his brother-in-law was one of the owners of the boat. He helped re-build the boat so that it would be able to make the long journey on the Gulf of Thailand.

"We left on December 18, 1978, and ended up in Malaysia a few days later," he said.

When they arrived at Malaysia the police weren't going to let them land because the country was already flooded with refugees.

"Our boat wouldn't have made another long trip, so we debated what to do," Minh said. "Finally we decided to ram the boat into the shore so that it wouldn't float anymore."

Minh and the others then asked for temporary asylum. They were then placed in a crowded refugee camp ten miles off the coast of Malaysia. There were more than 26,000 at the camp when they arrived.

"Two months after we arrived a group of Americans from voluntary agencies came to the island," Minh said. "One of them was John Bunch, one of the men I had worked with at the embassy."

John reassured Minh that his family would get to go to the United States, but he did warn that it was going to take awhile to get processed.

He was right. Minh and his family spent a total of seven months at the refugee camp.

During his time at the camp, Minh worked as a translator for United States personnel, Canadians, Australians and United Nations High Commission of Refugees.

Finally one day it was announced on the camp intercom that Minh and his family was going to be part of a group to get on a plane to head for the United States. This time he wasn't willing to give up his seat.

"I used to think about missing the helicopters," he said, "but I eventually just had to forget about it."

Minh had been upset about missing his chance to be evacuated so the first thing he did while in the United States was go to the library to read the press accounts of the final days in Saigon.

"I read the accounts and better understood that they didn't have a complete evacuation plan," he said. "That made me feel better."

After arriving in the United States he was sponsored by a Lutheran pastor from Webster, SD. Minh initially worked for a local plumbing and heating contractor.

"At that time 10,000 Vietnamese boat people were coming here every month," Minh said. "I told my sponsor that somewhere they must need someone like me."

He took Minh to Lutheran Social Services in Minneapolis and was told that Minh needed a driver's license before they could hire him. He then went back to Webster to learn how to drive a car.

During the fall of 1979 he received a call from Lutheran Social Services in Moorhead offering Minh a job. The job was provisional that he gets a driver's license. He started work on December 3, 1979. He has been working there ever since.

"When I first arrived in America I used to have nightmares about my time in prison," he said. "I have no regrets. I especially like my job working with refugees. It is rewarding to bring families back together."

Despite having gone though several severe hardships Minh has remained upbeat. Although he had to live in two refugee camps, one prison and attend re-education camp he views them as defining moments in his quest for freedom.

(Minh is in charge of refugee resettlement for Lutheran Social Services of Moorhead, Minnesota)

The Polar Bear
By
A Lutheran Pastor from North Dakota

This is a story of a new beginning in the middle of my life. I have heard the stories of silly men going kind of nuts when they hit middle age, desperately trying to deny the loss of youth. That would certainly never happen to me.

I had a great life, a beautiful family and a vocation in which I was able to use my gifts with joy. I had several very satisfying hobbies. I had goals and dreams. I had good health. Everything was fine. Middle age crisis? Not me!

As my kids grew toward adulthood and began more and more to exert their own wills and go their own ways, I got more and more uncomfortable. It was, of course, a gradual, insidious thing. I would try to be the dad that I had been to my kids when they were little, but they weren't little anymore. There was tension over that and my response was to retreat into myself – my hobbies mostly. I just kept more and more busy in my workshop and at my computer.

I have a tendency to be compulsive, but now it was becoming a real problem. If I wasn't working on some project I was obsessively thinking about it. I was just separating myself from my children who were having the audacity to grow up and from my wife who couldn't seem to see things from my perspective. Without being conscious of it I was operating out of the assumption that since they resisted my control they didn't want me around anyway. I developed a selfish "my way or no way" attitude which was resulting in a very lonely kind of life.

I built a lot of stuff and I couldn't understand why everyone was not as excited as I was about my accomplishments. It disturbed me when my wife would say, "Why are you doing this?" Or, "Why are you spending so much time and energy on that?" or "How many of these do you think you need?" "Why not?" is all I could say. I know that she meant "why are you doing that instead of spending time with me and with your kids?"

There are some words in the marriage service that I have repeated many times. It is a kind of solemn warning to newlyweds who might think that things will always be as they are on their wedding day. "Because of sin, our age-old rebellion, gift of marriage can be overcast and the gift of the family can become a burden." That is exactly what it felt like to me. I was feeling bitter and sad and frustrated, and I wondered what was wrong. I didn't want to see myself as the problem, but there was part of me that knew that I had lost my way.

On a study leave I was at the seminary where I had prepared for ministry years ago. Just being back in that place filled me with nostalgia and a deep sadness. What happened to that young man so full of hopes and dreams and passion for life and ministry? How did I get into this rut?

One afternoon I took my mother to the conservatory at the Como Park zoo. We walked around enjoying the beautiful plants and flowers and then, because it was such a beautiful February day, I suggested that we walk over and see the animals. I don't really like to see animals all caged up as they are at that zoo, so I don't know why I suggested it.

As we entered one of the buildings there was a crowd gathered oohing and ahhing about something. It was the polar bear they were watching. He was all alone in his enclosure.

He would climb his rocks and then fall backward into the water and swim one powerful stroke toward the glass through which we watched. He would bank off that glass and glide back to the place where he had started, climb those rocks and fall back into the water and do it all again. It was impressive—that huge beautiful beast so close that I could look right in his desperate eyes.

People would watch this spectacle for a while with delight until they realized that it was an elaborate pacing routine. Then you could hear them say, "That's sad!" It was sad indeed. This beautiful creature meant to live free in the world not even enjoying the relative freedom of his fairly good-sized enclosure. That's so sad, I thought, and that's me!

I prayed a desperate kind of prayer that night as I lay awake wondering how to get a new start. I confessed my brokenness in a way that I hadn't for a long time because I had not let myself be aware of it. I asked God to lead me into a renewal of my faith and a new way of being in my family and all aspects of my life. I was afraid that it was too late, that maybe I had gotten too hard inside. Here I was the man of God who boldly proclaimed God's grace and love for others wondering if it could be real for me.

That was the beginning of what I have come to see as going around a wide curve in the road. I think we all would prefer to just turn the corner, but deep lasting change takes time. It's not easy to change. What I needed at that point and still today was not just chicken soup for my soul. There's nothing wrong with chicken soup, but sometimes we need something more like red-hot chili peppers for our souls.

First, I had to confess my failures to myself and then to God and then to my wife and my kids. I had to ask for forgiveness and begin, with God's help, to act in more loving and mature ways. I had to give up my compulsive striving and my isolation (my pacing), which for the most part has not been difficult because I enjoy a new kind of relationship with my family and friends and with God. I am clinging to God these days in a way that I didn't when I was blind to my need.

Every once in a while I think of that polar bear pacing his cage, and I thank God that it doesn't have to be that way. We can, as the answer to that little warning in the marriage service says, "be sustained in our weariness and have our joy restored." Thanks be to God!

"You will know the truth, and the truth will make you free."   John 8:32

The Lesson
By
Caline Olson

There had been a death in her family. Not the devastating, gut-wrenching death of a parent but a death and a loss just the same. Her mother had given birth to a stillborn little boy.

Ali was a second grader. As her P.E. teacher, I wasn't prepared to deal with it. There were no classes in college that prepared me for situations like this. No "Death of Student's Family Members 101." Like most people, I had always had trouble expressing sympathy to bereaved adults. How could I possibly find words to comfort a little girl?

I knew that a lot of children Ali's age would have acted to the tragedy with indifference. Their innocence would have protected them, but Ali was different. She was quiet, reserved and thoughtful. She was the protective, motherly type. She already had a three-year-old brother and I had observed the way she hovered over him, indulged him, basked in his boyish rambunctiousness.

I knew just how she was looking forward to a new baby sister or brother. She had talked of the event for months now. She would come up to me in that quiet manner of hers, tug on my arm and say, "Teacher, my mom is going to have our baby pretty soon."

On Friday, with the pink blush of anticipation stamped on her cheeks and Fourth of

July sparklers for eyes, she had told me, "My mom went to the hospital this morning to have our new baby."

On Saturday I learned of the baby's death. On Monday Ali wasn't in school. I learned there had been a family burial service.

I knew that Ali would be back to school on Tuesday. What words of comfort would I have for her? My mind raced. I worried, I planned, I rehearsed and I worried some more. In spite of my dread, Tuesday came and with it second grade P.E. class.

When the students burst through the gym door that afternoon, I only had eyes for Ali. I saw immediately the pain of her loss. She shuffled as the others skipped or ran to their designated spots. Her eyes were fixed on her feet.

She came straight to me, "Teacher, I have a tummy ache. Can I sit out today?"

"Of course," was all I said, letting the opportunity to comfort and console her slip by. She slithered along to the bleachers and slumped to the floor oblivious to what was going on around her. I got the activities going, gathered up my courage and went to her.

This was it. I must say something now. I sat down beside her.

Just as I was drawing a deep breath in getting ready to begin, I saw D.J. skipping rope toward us.

"Oh, no!" I thought to myself as he took a running leap and slid up to us like a baseball star sliding into home plate. "Not D.J. Not now."

D.J. was all boy—freckles and sweat and rumpled hair. He did everything in high gear and he had only one volume—loud.

He made me smile and I loved him dearly, but at this particular moment I would have loved him more on the opposite side of the gym.

"Hi, Ali!" He blurted out. "Your baby brother died, huh?"

"Yeah," Ali whispered.

"Gee, I bet that made you feel sad. What happened to him anyway?"

"My mom said he didn't get enough air or something when he was born. So he died. But she said he's in heaven now and that will be his home."

"Gosh, I bet you cried, huh?"

"Yeah."

"Well, it's a good thing you still have your other brother to play with! He's cute and funny! Ya wanna jump rope with me?"

"OK."

"Come on."

They skipped off D.J. sweating and plowing his way through the other second graders; Ali giggling and tagging along behind him. It made me smile.

I understood that for perhaps the thousandth time since I had begun teaching I had learned something invaluable from my students.

The lesson was over. The healing had begun out of the mouths of babes.

(Caline is a lifelong educator)

Faith Shaping Experience
By
Tim Bauer

    Steve, the oldest of the boys, was almost four years older than I was. He was big in body, bold in action and was determined to make things happen the way he thought best. Even though we had numerous disputes, sibling fights and attempts to get each other in trouble, I loved and respected my brother.

    One person with whom Steve never seemed to blend with was my father. They seemed to never agree on anything, whether it be plowing a cornfield or buying a car. Steve wasn't disrespectful, but he wasn't going to give in to the instructions of my father without making his opinions known.

    As long as I could remember these two had never gotten along with each other. I also recall my father and brother yelling at each other in the machine shed during harvest. As they tried to work together in order to prepare and repair harvest equipment, their voices rang loud and distinct with harsh and profane words through the crisp, clear fall air.

    After graduating from high school, Steve enlisted in the US Army. He headed off for training and deployment into the Vietnam War. He would write home a couple times each month. However, I never noticed my father reading his letters. Nor did I ever see my father add any notes or even his signature to the letters that our family sent back to Steve on the other side of the world. However, with Steve away from the farm it was noticeably quieter. Maybe my father didn't have anyone with which to argue or possibly he was thinking about his role as father to a son that may never again come home.

Following two years in the Vietnam War, Steve returned home. Our whole family (father included) went to the Minneapolis Airport to welcome Steve home. He was safe and relatively unharmed from his time in combat. As Steve and I became reacquainted, I could tell that he had changed. He wasn't as big, bold, or brash as I had remembered. I'm not sure if this was due to changes in Steve or in myself. Nevertheless, it was a delight to enter into a new relationship with my brother. It was only a couple of months before Steve moved away again. He began to pursue a degree at the University of Minnesota, focusing in the area of forestry and natural resources. The brother who I once thought might be satisfied taking over the farm was out to explore a new vocation. It was an exciting time in my life and my relationship with Steve!

From my perceptions, Steve and my father were congenial with one another following his return from Vietnam. Yet, I hadn't noticed any change in their relationship. They weren't yelling at one another because they weren't working together. My father knew that Steve wasn't going to stay on the farm, but instead pursue other options for life. In the midst of all of these changes there really didn't seem to be any changes between them. It appeared that a mutual truce had become a reality without either person speaking to the other.

One year at the University of Minnesota was behind him and Steve was back on the farm for the summer. He connected with some high school friends. They enjoyed time and recreation together. It was a Wednesday in August when Steve and about 20 of his friends headed off for an afternoon of canoeing. Later that evening we received a call from Steve's closest friend that he was missing.

Steve had been canoeing with various people throughout the afternoon. He was last seen when the group stopped for a lunch break. It was assumed that Steve journeyed on with another canoe. However, when everyone finished the trip, Steve was nowhere to be found. The owner of the canoe rental business was notified. We all assumed that Steve would appear on Thursday after having been lost in the woods next to the river overnight.

Early the next day my father and I went to the home of the owner of the canoe rental business. The owner was concerned about what had happened, but wasn't expressing any sense of tragedy.

He had called the county sheriff to see if a search of the area could occur. My father was in agreement with the search. The two of them chatted with one another, sharing a variety of information. Finally the telephone rang. It was the sheriff, telling the owner of the canoe business and then my father that Steve's body had been found in the river. Steve had drowned.

Immediately my father began sobbing. This soon turned into crying, then wailing. I was overcome with what I was seeing. In the eighteen years that I had lived, I had never seen my father cry.

Even when he broke his forearm while trying to start a tractor, never a tear was shed. But now this man whom I remembered yelling at Steve, not signing letters to Vietnam, and not expressing support or surprise in Steve's decision to go to college was overpowered by the reality of death.

What I saw wasn't a weak man, or someone feeling sorry for himself. I instead saw a father who deeply loved his son, even though the relationship had never been openly friendly.

I saw a tough father doubled up by the reality that he would never be able to express his love for his son. I was brought to the ultimate reality that my father deeply loved his first son, even though everything I had seen up to this point gave no indication of the depth of that relationship.

Over the years I have recalled this vision time and again. I have learned that perceptions aren't always accurate. Nor does love have to be openly and frequently expressed for it to be solid and significant.

In my understanding of relationships and faithfulness what I saw in my father reinforces the fact that the love between God and creation, between God and I, goes beyond the surface into the very depths of existence.

(Tim is a Lutheran Pastor for two congregations in Northwestern Minnesota. He is also a chaplain for the Hospice of the Red River Valley)

Don't Ever Judge a Book by Its Cover
By
Chad A. Filley

Throughout the years I have dealt with thousands of youth. Some have maturity far beyond their years while others seem to struggle to act their age. Too often I've seen rebellious youth experiment with things that they know are wrong, but still misbehave just too shock parents or impress friends.

On rare occasions I have dealt with youth that just don't look like they are going to make it. It could be due to their background or their lifestyle, but either way it just doesn't look like they have what it takes to succeed. Here's a story about one of those youth.

A friend of mine called me one day to see if I could intervene with one of the teenage girls that worked at her daycare center. Susan gave me quite an extensive sketch of the girl's background and from what she told me I decided that it would be a good idea for the three of us to meet on neutral ground.

Susan told me that the girl was sixteen years old, loved to party, slept around with any guy that smiled at her, was thinking of dropping out of school and hated any type of organized religion. The girl was obviously on a crash course with trouble.

We decided to meet in the middle of the afternoon at one of the fast food restaurants in town. It's surprising how quiet these restaurants are during off-peak times.

Susan walked in first and was followed by a tall, strikingly beautiful girl. The first thing I noticed about this girl as she approached was that her beauty seemed to fade away the closer she got. It was obvious that this teenager had seen some hard road. Her left eye had an extensive amount of makeup that unsuccessfully tried to cover up a black eye. Someone had hit her.

As I was getting to know Angie she blurted out "I'm sixteen and I've slept with sixteen guys."

I'm not certain if she revealed this more to shock me or in an attempt to impress me, but either way it was one of the more bizarre comments I'd heard.

"Are you going to keep this streak up until you are eighty?" I asked her hoping to let her see how ridiculous this comment had been.

After staring at me for awhile trying to decide what angle I was coming from she said "I like this guy. He's cool."

Soon after that she told me that she had a problem that she needed to work through.

"I'm in love with two guys and I can't decide which one I want to be with," she told me.

On the surface this sounded like a good dilemma, but as she explained more I got a true sense of just how dysfunctional her frame of mind truly was.

She began telling me about her first boyfriend and eventually revealed that he was the one that had given her the black eye. He had found out about her dating the second boy and had gotten violent with her.

"Isn't it neat how much he loves me," she said.

As she began telling me about the second man in her life I figured he had to be better than the first one. Boy, was I wrong. She disclosed that they had met at a party. She had too much to drink and eventually passed out. Being the Good Samaritan that he was he offered to take her home. On the way to her house he pulled off onto a side road and took advantage of her.

"I can't decide which one I like better," she said, "They're both so neat."

I could hardly believe my ears. This screwed up little girl was having trouble deciding which one she liked better, the one that raped her or the one that beat her.

The more she said the more depressed I got. She also disclosed growing up in a dysfunctional family that made it obvious why her life was something short of normal.

After about an hour of talking I decided that we would meet again in a few day after I had a chance to get some numbers of counseling services for her.

As I drove off I couldn't help but pity this girl. She just seemed like she had too many strikes against her. Although I had only known her for a short while I had a hard time believing that she was ever going to lead a very successful or productive life.

How could she? She had been abused as a young child. She was at the whim of every male who decided she was worth the little effort required to have sex with her. She had little to no self-esteem and was acting out in some of the most damaging ways possible for a teenager. What kind of a future was in store for her?

Things like this depress me. I have always been saddened when I see someone that never really got a fair shake. It reminded me of the time I was in the Twin Cities going through training for youth ministry. One of our assignments was to go door to door and evangelize to people. It was assumed that if we could do this then we could certainly minister to the youth at our church.

It's amazing the amount of diversity that can live in one single neighborhood. I remember encountering an atheist and a Jehovah's Witness among many others. Imagine a Lutheran knocking on the door of a Jehovah's Witness to talk about religion.

Of all the people my partner and I encountered there was one that still haunts me. This man lived in the alley behind the nice house on the street. He was sitting in a pair of bib overalls and was holding a bottle of beer.

"You guys ain't selling anything are you?"

We assured him that we were only going around to talk about God and he stopped us in mid-sentence.

"You might as well stop. I ain't been to church since Sunday school and I've lived an evil life. My mother always told me I would never amount to anything. She was right. Not even Jesus could love someone like me."

The two of us tried to tell the man that Jesus could and did love someone like him, but it was of no use. We were wasting our breath. This man was suffering a living hell of self-despair.

I hadn't thought of this man for quite awhile, but seeing someone like Angie brought back the same feelings of pity that I had for him.

I decided that I would meet Susan and Angie at the daycare center where they worked. I got there a little early and had a chance to observe Angie interact with the young children. She was amazing!

I couldn't believe that this was the same girl. She handled them masterfully. She was definitely gifted. In the short time I was there she handled a dispute over a toy between two children, she bandaged up a young boy that had scraped his knee and she handled all of the others with an amazing level of maturity and patience.

She also interacted well with all of the parents as they came to pick up their children. Before each parent left she informed him or her of at least one good thing the child had done during the day. Every child hugged her on the way out the door. It was impressive.

After witnessing this I no longer pitied Angie. I had just witnessed her performing her own type of ministry. She was sharing unconditional love with these children in a way that not everyone would be able to.

Angie did seek out the needed counseling to help her deal with her issues, but she also taught me a very valuable lesson when dealing with youth. Don't ever judge a book by its cover. Cliché or not this is true.

If I had classified Angie as being hopeless I probably wouldn't have fought as hard as I did to get her to see a counselor. I probably would have given up on her. What a mistake that would have been.

> Angie is a compilation of many different youth. This story is told not to single out a specific incident, but instead to show a defining lesson I learned while working with youth. I learned to judge people according to their inner qualities and not on outward appearances.

Heartsick
By
Caline Olson

It was springtime. I know this because while I was in the hospital, one of my brothers had his first communion, which was held in early June, and when my dad came to visit me, he was usually dressed in his work clothes. He smelled of wet, turned-over earth. I loved the way he smelled and having him there in the room with me was almost like getting to go outside.

It was springtime—a busy time. Life is so insistent in springtime. It races. It pushes. It forces its way up and out, and I had been sentenced to a hospital bed. Springtime and life itself were leaving me behind.

I was eleven. It was the end of my fifth grade year in school. My classmates sent me get well cards. I still have them—crumbled and faded and glued into a scrapbook.

Strep throat had run rampant through my family and in its wake had left three of us with secondary infections that attacked the linings of our hearts. I don't remember feeling sick—only tired. When my little sister Ketter and I complained incessantly of our legs aching, Dad took us to the doctor, and the viral thief robbing us of energy was discovered.

I remember the scurrying of getting the two of us checked into the hospital and tucked into our hospital beds. At first it seemed like a great adventure. We had each other for familiarity when everything around us was strange and unfamiliar. For those first hours and days Ketter was my security.

At home I had lots of brothers and sisters to mother—to hold and kiss and take care of. In that cold, sterile hospital environment, Ketter was my link to them. Though we were confined to our beds, we were at least in the same room in the west end of the hospital.

I clung to her across the five-foot gap between our beds. I could fall asleep comforted by the fact that she was there. She was five and exceptionally brave. I don't recall that she ever cried. I do remember that without fail when I woke up in the morning or from a nap, she was sitting up in her bed with a blanket in her lap watching me with her big, brown eyes.

Doctors and nurses came in to examine us. They exclaimed the rarity of this heart condition and the unlikelihood of it attacking three children in the same family. They talked above us and over us and around us but not to us. When they poked and prodded Ketter she would lock her eyes on mine and with my thought locked on hers I would mother her through the exam. Nothing was said out loud. My mothering was telepathic. Never do I remember that she cried, and so I didn't either. I swallowed the homesickness down an aching throat past a broken heart.

We were confined to those beds, and so bedpans became part of our daily routine. I would buzz for a nurse's aide when I had to go.

Ketter would tell me when she had to go and I would buzz and say, "My sister has to go to the bathroom."

One heavy, ponderous aide seemed particularly resentful about my buzzing, and when she was on duty, we would hold ourselves to the point of pain. One day she shuffled in mumbling under her breath that we certainly weren't that sick and that she couldn't understand doctor's orders that forbade us to get up and go to the bathroom.

"These doctors don't know what they are doing," she mumbled.

I took her word for it and began getting up and sneaking into the bathroom to relieve myself. I would help Ketter with her bedpan when she had to go. I was willing to take the chance with my own health and risk the run to the bathroom on the other side of the room, but I wasn't willing to take a chance with Ketter's. My heart lurched and squeaked and complained but not nearly as much as that nurse had.

I was smart enough to buzz for the bedpans occasionally. I realized that no calls would arouse suspicions. I hoped to stave off a full-blown investigation. Either the nurses didn't care or didn't keep track because no one ever became concerned about what must have been a world record case of constipation.

Ketter was my link to love and after ten days they sent her home. I was glad for her. I had to be glad for her, but I didn't want her to go. As I write this, I remember and feel again that ache in my throat and chest as I sat and smiled and waved goodbye from that bed when they took her away. She was leaving me. I was alone. They were all leaving me.

There weren't other children in the hospital. Babies are born occasionally in small towns but not regularly. Sometimes weeks and even months go by without a birth. And children are healthy. They don't get hospitalized. When Ketter went home they moved me to the east end of the hospital.

Sometimes I had roommates. They were not children. They were cases of female problems that I didn't understand. The nurses and doctors were secretive about what ailed those patients. They were never roommates for very long.

They all had procedures. One young red-haired woman had her procedure in the morning, and when she got up to go to the bathroom in the afternoon, she fainted on the floor. I buzzed and buzzed as she moaned and groaned at the foot of my bed. I watched and wondered about the mysteries of womanhood as they put her back into bed. She went home the next morning.

Another woman stayed for almost a week. She had a procedure called a hysterectomy. I had no clue what that meant. She was kind—more grandmotherly than motherly. I was enthralled and enchanted by her family when they came to visit. She had a husband and a son. The son could actually come into the hospital room and visit, and he wasn't even grown-up. He was sixteen. Hospital rules allowed no one under sixteen to visit which, of course, included all of my brothers and sisters.

I watched this tiny family and marveled. There were only three of them. What would that be like? There were eight of us—ten counting mom and dad. What would it be like to have a big brother? I daydreamed about it and decided I wanted one. A big brother would come and see me. He would take care of me and be my protector—my knight in shining armor. I pretended that these three were my family. The woman gave me a gift the day she went home. I don't remember what it was. I do remember that she looked at me with such pity when she gave it to me that I wanted to cry. I didn't cry.

It wasn't that I didn't have any visitors. I did. Dad always stopped when he came to town for seed or machinery parts or some other farm supplies. He smelled so wonderful—like the outdoors. He always brought me something to eat—a chocolate malt, or a bunch of bananas or candy. He couldn't stay long. He was busy...springtime busy.

He would leave. I would choke down whatever he brought and it would get stuck in my throat. I wasn't able to get them past the lump of homesickness. They were often salted with tears. It got so I didn't want Dad to come. The pain of his leaving seemed to outweigh the joy of his coming.

Of course, on Sundays, the whole family could stop. At least the part of the family that made it to Sunday Mass—Dad and the bigger kids. They would stop, and if the right nurse was on duty, I would be allowed to walk down the corridor to the waiting room to say hello. My little brothers and sisters seemed to stare at their sick big sister. They were anxious to get away from this smelly place. It was springtime. They were racing and pushing and forcing their way up and out. Seeing them in that hospital environment really only made things worse. They were out of their element.

My step-grandmother, Grandma Ruth, visited me and brought an Etch-a-Sketch. I became an expert at Etch-a-Sketch design. She taught me games of solitaire, which occupied my time for many hours in the months to come. She would show me a game and then let me try to play it on my own. Invariably, I would win the first time.

"Now you're hooked," she exclaimed. "Solitaire is the devil's game!"

One day she convinced the nurses to let me go down the corridor to a bookshelf where I was able to pick out some books to read. I remember lying in bed and reading for endless hours until my arms and neck ached from the discomfort of holding the book up. I stopped only when the exertion reached a point where my heart squeaked and squealed so loudly that I could not concentrate anymore.

One day after a marathon reading session the doctor stopped on his rounds, and when he stepped through the door, he said, "Listen." He and the nurse accompanying him marveled at how they could hear the hammering, squeaking heart across the room—audible without the use of a stethoscope.

I read horse books—<u>Black Beauty</u> and others. The stories took me away from that hospital bed into worlds of adventure. One book, <u>Freckles</u>, caused me such pain that I shall never forget it. The main character, a redheaded boy named Freckles, dies. It was the first book that I had ever read that made me cry. It also made me worry. I couldn't die could I? Surely little girls with heart conditions didn't die? I also worried that the doctors would make me stop reading.

I recognized that the reading strained my heart—much more than sneaking to the bathroom ever had. Fortunately the nurses and doctors didn't notice.

I will always be grateful to Grandma Ruth for the time she took to find activities for me that passed the time away. Yes, Grandma Ruth came to visit. Grandma Rasmussen, the grandmother I really loved, didn't. I excused her. It was springtime. She was busy.

The nights were the worst—the evening hours from six to nine. The loneliness then was almost unbearable. Some nurses and aides gave backrubs before bedtime, and those backrubs were the best medicine that I got. The bed rest and the penicillin were not nearly so therapeutic as the miracle of those backrubs. I know. It was, after all, my heart. I knew its rhythms. And always after a backrub, it was quieted and stopped trying to burst through the walls of my chest.

My condition didn't worsen, but it didn't improve either. Dr. Klaussen visited daily—sometimes twice daily—on his hospital rounds. He had consulted a pediatrician in far away Jamestown for advice. Dr. Miles, a children's heart specialist, had recommended the regimen of bed rest and penicillin that had been prescribed. On his visits, Dr. Klaussen listened to my heart. When I heard him coming down the hall giving instructions to the RN with him about what to do for this patient and that patient, I willed my heart to be well. Even though there were times that it rested quietly and beat regularly before his arrival, by the time he entered the room, it had decided to defy me.

It defied me and squeaked out its message, "I'm sick. I'm sick. I'm sick." I willed it to be well.

"How are you today?" he would ask.

"I'm well!" I would respond.

He lifted my hospital gown and moved the lie detector's cold metal ear from place to place on my chest and back.

"Not yet. You're not well yet," he would say.

I knew. I heard my defiant heart squeak. I felt it rubbing and grating. I knew that I should be grateful that at least I didn't feel sick, but I didn't feel grateful. I felt cursed and betrayed by my own heart. I wanted to get up and go out. I wanted to play. So went the daily ritual of the exam.

Enough was enough. I longed for a break in the sameness of the days. They woke me at seven, brought me breakfast at eight and I tried to stave off boredom for the next three hours while waiting in eagerness and dread of the ritual exam. They brought me lunch at noon, made me nap at one and I dealt with boredom of the afternoon. They brought me supper at five-thirty and sometimes there was another ritualistic exam followed by the unbearable hours between six and nine; they turned the lights out at nine-thirty. Each day the same. I longed for a break in the sameness.

I do remember two unusual happenings. One night at 8 p.m. I got a bloody nose. I was embarrassed about getting blood all over my bed, but I couldn't stop it on my own. I buzzed and the nurses tried a variety of methods to stop the bleeding—direct pressure, ice packs. Nothing worked. Nothing slowed the rhythmical gushing of blood. I could taste it as it ran down my throat, when at last, I threw up the blood I had been swallowing. The nurses got excited and called the doctor. It was nearly ten when he came hurrying in.

Funny how I could smell with a broken nose just like I could feel with a broken heart. He rushed in and when he bent over me, I could smell his house and his family on his clothes. I wondered about his life away from the hospital. I felt guilty for pulling him away from it. He stuffed my nose with what seemed like a truckload of gauze and told me that breathing was going to be difficult or at least a little different since I would be doing it through my mouth. He promised me I would be OK by morning.

When he came in the next morning on his rounds, he mercifully pulled the stuffing from my nose and pronounced my nose cured. I noticed that he smelled his usual medicinal self.

Another morning perhaps three weeks into my stay, Dr. Klaussen came in and found me scratching my head.

"Does your head itch?" he asked. As I nodded an affirmative, he bent closer and sniffed. "Have the nurses washed your hair since you have been here?" he queried.

"Ugh, ugh," I responded.

Abruptly he left the room. I heard his raised voice directed at the nurses down the hall. Not ten minutes later I was treated to a shampoo in bed.

The same day I got my hair shampooed two other exciting things happened. On his evening rounds Dr. Klaussen made the pronouncement that I so longed to hear, "I think you're getting well. If things continue to improve, maybe you can go home on Sunday."

I didn't hear the "maybe." All I heard was the word "home" and the promise of Sunday. That I was improving didn't matter. That Dr. Klaussen had been moved by pity to throw a morsel of hope to a poor little waif with smelly hair didn't occur to me. The promise of home loomed before me. My grating, grumbling heart squeaked out a single note of joy. Had Dr.

Klaussen heard the crying turn to singing as I felt the shift in tone?

Right after he left my room, the patient down the hall shuffled by in her bathrobe and slippers pushing a mobile IV unit before her. Evidently, she had been pronounced well enough to walk the halls by the benevolent Dr. Klaussen. As she passed by my open door, I transferred my joy to her. I smiled and waved.

When she came back by on her return, I smiled and waved again and she came shuffling in. She asked me who I was and why I was in the hospital. I happily gave out the details finishing with, "But I'm getting well and I'll be going home on Sunday."

She told me who she was and that she was from Marion, a small town twenty-six miles north of LaMoure. She was in the hospital for some procedure—some surgical procedure. She too would be going home on Sunday. I fairly beamed at her—Little Miss Sunshine sparkling up and out of the white sheets. She asked about the playing cards on my bedside table. Before she left she asked if it would be OK if she came in sometimes and played cards with me.

I beamed up at her, "Yeah! Sure!"

Bedtime didn't seem so bad that night.

The next few days crawled by. I spent lots of time just looking at the clock willing it to move faster. Each minute that ticked mercifully by meant I was that much closer to the promise of home. My only time out from clock watching came when the lady from Marion came in each morning, afternoon and evening to play cards with me. We became fast friends. We had been thrown together in confinement and would be set free on Sunday. We laughed and played together to wile away the time. We were comrades, compatriots, and cellmates. I loved her for her kindness and willingness to share those endless hours of anticipation with me. I was getting well. I was going home on Sunday.

Sunday finally came. I was bursting with eagerness. If my hospital gown hadn't had a slit down the back, I would have burst at the seams. At eleven Dr. Klaussen came in. He performed the ritualistic exam; posed the question, "How are you today?"

"I'm well." All the while he listened through the stethoscope that had suddenly become my ally, my mind sang, "I'm going home. I'm going home. I'm going home."

But I heard it even as I denied it. I heard it as it denied me.

"I'm sick. I'm sick. I'm sick," my heart squeaked out its rhythmical betrayal.

"I'm well! I'm well! I'm going home!" my mind screamed.

His hand rested on my shoulder. He leaned forward and closed his eyes in concentration. Then he raised his eyes to mine and pronounced his sentence, "Not yet. You're not quite well yet. Maybe you can go home on Wednesday. Maybe Wednesday."

Before the shock wore off, he was gone. I sat in stunned disbelief as my heart and mind screamed at each other. The sob could not be stifled. The tears would not be denied. They gathered ferociously in my eyes. They welled up and out. They spilled onto the hospital gown that sheathed my forever broken heart. Little Miss Sunshine was reduced to a hopelessly blubbering puddle cowering down and under the white sheets.

I heard the shuffling of her slippered feet. I grabbed a book from my bed stand and hid my swollen, tortured face.

"Hi. What are you doing?"

"Reading."

"Good book?"

"Ah huh."

"Just came in to say goodbye. I'll be going home in a little while."

The words on the pages before me were a blur. A continuous, unstoppable river of tears rolled over my cheeks, cascading to my chest. I choked back the sobs and let my nose drip unheeded.

"I wanted to tell you how much I enjoyed our card games. You are such a nice," her voice broke, "such a nice little girl."

I didn't look. I couldn't look.

"I'll write you a letter. You'll probably be home before it gets here."

I didn't speak. I couldn't speak.

"Goodbye. Be seeing ya." She reached out and squeezed my foot beneath the white sheet. She shuffled out. Had I looked—had I dared to look, I would surely have seen that hope was going with her.

I cried. I cried on and on. At some point the nurse named Marion came in. She took pity on me. To this day I consider her a saint. I have always wanted to let her know how important her act of kindness was. I believe that it saved a little girl's life. She washed my face with a cool washcloth and washed my soul with soothing words, "Would you like to go down the hall and look at the new baby in the nursery?"

I mustered a nod.

"Well, then, we'll just hike you down there to take a look." And as big as I was and as tiny as she was, she gathered me up in her arms and carried me down to that nursery.

I don't remember anything after that. I either cannot or do not wish to. I know that in approximately another week I did go home. But for the life of me, I can't remember. I don't know why I can't remember. I've tried. I just can't. Maybe someday I will remember. Maybe memories are like life in the springtime. They are insistent. They race. They push and eventually they force their way up and out.

(Caline is a lifelong educator)

Career Change
By
Charles Yue

Have you ever wondered why someone with a dream job and a matching salary would give it all up? Charles Yue did just that and he doesn't regret it one bit. Here is his story.

I was born in Shanghai, the largest city in China. The year was 1951; just two years after the Communists came into power. Due to the political situation at that time, I was separated from my father and older siblings until I was five when the family was reunited in Hong Kong where I spent my school years. Throughout my childhood, I suffered from many severe health problems that restricted both my physical activities and social environment. As a result, I grew up as a quiet and private kid very close to my mother who eventually nursed me to health, but with few intimate friends and regrettably disengaged from my father whom I hardly came to know. My mother was a wise and courageous woman with much self-control and dignity, while my father was an upright and honorable man with great self-discipline and a sense of responsibility. They were totally committed to each other and dedicated all their energies to raising their children to have meaningful and productive lives. I inherited the more traditionally feminine qualities of home economics and the art of human relations from my mother, while I learned problem-solving disciplines and the joy of life-long learning from my father's examples. I was indeed blessed with an upbringing that now serves as a model for myself as a parent.

Although my parents were atheists, who had much contempt for religious practices, they sent all their children to parochial schools only for the quality of the education being offered there. Spirituality was discouraged at home and church attendance was limited to being invited by friends to Christmas and Easter celebrations.

Naturally, religion was part of the school curriculum, and I remember that while I did not care much about catechism, I was fascinated by the stories of individual encounter with God in the Bible -- life experiences that I could personally relate to at an intimate spiritual level.

Thus began my "lifelong" respect for the Scriptures and a passionate desire to know the Lord, although the discipline to study the Word had yet to be cultivated in me. Eventually but through the grace of God, we all came to believe in the name of Jesus -- including my parents! After years of prayers and sharing of faith with love, it was none other than their children who led them to receive Christ into their hearts and lives before they left homeward bound for the place the Lord had prepared for them (John 14:2-3).

In 1969, I came to the United States to pursue a college education in engineering, but instead came to the realization that human technology is inadequate to solve human problems. In my quest for answers to life's questions, God met me at my acknowledged needs, and I started my life journey in faith on April 13, 1973.

Immediately, I was put to the test with disappointments in personal relationships, and the disruptions in my life as I left for home to attend to my father's terminal illness and other family affairs. When I returned two years later, I felt abandoned by the world and harbored much resentment. My faith based on belief in a revealed truth was like the seed that fell on the rock (Luke 8:13).

In my determination to prove myself to the world, I resorted to self-reliance and managed to impress many people with my "success" including graduate degrees, an advancing career in business and financial independence. However, I was not fooling myself with my inner spiritual void. Without trust in a revealed God, there was no faith!

Jesus said that He came so that we may have life and have it abundantly (John 10:10). A life worth His dying for is a life worth my living for. So like the prodigal son, I came to myself, got up, went to my Father, and asked for the privilege of being one of His servants (Luke 15:17-19).

In due course, I abandoned the lifestyle of a corporate executive and re-established my priorities. My life directive now reads: "To serve God faithfully in His calling as He fills my days with His peace and joy. To always be true to myself in living a life to the full; to be an example of courage for many and make the difference in the lives of a few." Above all, the Lord has blessed me with the joy in knowing Him more and more, the desire to grow in Him, and the opportunity to go and share Him with whom He draws to me (John 14:6).

I have been humbled to begin this walk with Christ at home, in becoming a more loving husband to Mary Jane my wife of over twenty years, and a more effective parent to the five happy and healthy children God has blessed us with.

In 1988, I started a consulting practice in human development to cultivate personal effectiveness and servant leadership by building motivation, character and discipline within the individual. In the process, I was affirmed of some special giftedness and experienced much personal satisfaction in the area of counseling. With a heart to help bring about real meaning and relevance in the lives of others, I was encouraged to complete my graduate work in counseling psychology in 1994.

Currently, I am maintaining my balance both in leadership and as a practitioner in the field of inner healing and spiritual regeneration. Aside from serving as a college president for a graduate school of professional psychology, I continue in my eighth year of counseling ministry working with individuals and their families on spirituality, abuse, relationship and family-of-origin issues.

While I am uncertain what the future holds—whether in education, counseling or ministry, what I am certain is who holds the future. For now, I am content to set my heart straight (Ezra 7:10) and to do what the Lord requires of me (Micah 6:8).

Hometown Reminiscence
By
Thomas Jefferson

I recently had an opportunity to visit my hometown. I've been toying with the idea of doing a story of my journey that would include how I came to be where I am, my story and what made me the way I am. This trip was special in other ways also. It gave me a chance to bond with my mother in such a way that we hadn't for quite some time, and it helped to bring me in touch with people and places that meant something to me.

The end of a five-hundred mile trip put me in Columbia, South Carolina, my birthplace where I was reminded of so many things that would have been impossible to recall if I were not in that city. There is something special about Columbia and the whole state of South Carolina. Columbia is the capitol and there is a major controversy surrounding the flag that flies above the capitol building, it's flown there since 1962.

The year 1962 is significant too, I finished high school and my family moved to Washington, DC. The phrase used at that time was "going north." Jacob Lawrence depicted it so clear in one of his art works, "The Great Migration". This period was described as the greatest industrial movement in the history of the U.S. It included a movement of Blacks from the rural south to industrial cities of the north, from field to factory, of which we were at the rear end of. I've said all the above to prepare you for understanding my story.

When I look back at my beginning I shouldn't have made it this far. I begin with slingshot pond, our old swimming-hole down along the Congoree River. My gang and I found great adventure exploring the riverbanks for wildlife for which we could kill. We found snakes, frogs, lizards, turtles and other things that could be fun to kill. Our favorite was dropping big rocks on turtles, to see if their backs could withstand the weight and force of rocks dropped on their backs. I don't know how we survived to love pets, after being so cruel during our youth. We just didn't know all the avenues of having fun without going after wild things.

Despite my backward way of having fun, I think I developed into a pretty good kid. I did many of the things that boys of those days did, such as selling newspapers, peanuts, working as a shoeshine boy, and picking cotton. I worked in all these different jobs because it helped my mom with my education expenses. It was customary in my family for the kids to work and help out with some of the household expenses, so I never thought it was unusual. Out of these experiences I learned some very valuable lessons that have become part of my character today. I learned the value of work as it relates to self worth, the importance of helping family, the value of money, fairness and the ability to work with others.

My journey has taken me from Columbia, S.C. to Washington, D.C., to Munich Germany, and eventually to Fargo, N.D. It doesn't seem possible that I would have come this far when I look back at such humble beginnings. I had no role models, my father was not around, having a divorced mother whom had to raise eight kids on a domestic's salary. I can only credit my mother for building character in me. And, the community (ghetto) where I lived was really like a village that raised all the children.

I never knew that we were poor until I left that community. My recent visit there was also a reminder of the pride all of the tenants had in taking care of their personal little plots. There is so much truth in the quote: "in order to know where you're going, you must know where you've been. I know, because I've been there, in that place where you had nothing. So when all is not well with me now, it's much easier to cope."

We arrived in Washington on one of those hot June days, in 1951 in a Junebug green, Lincoln, pulling a u-haul with all our possessions. We were ready to start a new life up north. It was exciting to me because I wasn't smart enough to realize the hardship my mother had to endure in having to find work and a place to live for a large family with no realistic direction.

My early experience in DC was new and exciting, everything and everybody gave me something of value. My first job was as a dishwasher at an area bowling alley working for a $1 per hour, but that was still a step up from what I got in South Carolina, half of that amount was my best. That first summer I must have had three jobs in four months, all in maintenance. I learned that I needed education if I ever wanted to have the opportunity to get better jobs. College was the only option, and I was off to prove that I could win a scholarship for my sports skills.

My sport of choice at that time was football, and I thought I was good, based on my star status in high school, however, that was short-lived, once I stepped on campus among all the other stars from their respective schools. I lasted one year and dropped out, because I didn't have any guidance or direction. I thought everything would just fall into place but I was wrong, one must make things happen. So I put my tail between my legs and headed back to DC.

This time I did have a somewhat better chance at landing a job that paid good money. I thought that I was moving on up, to borrow the theme song from the Jefferson's sitcom. I was on a path of learning a technical skill that shaped my working career for the next fifteen years. I worked in and learned the skilled trade of making printing inks, and some life skills at the same time, both negative and positive.

During those eight years at this printing ink company I met some of the wildest characters that I've ever met, then and now. It was here that I learned to party with boys, meaning we could go all night long, chasing, dancing, drinking, and howling at the moon from someone's backyard. We would then, race the sun home, the next morning, peering through the steering wheel and facing the morning sun. Some of us would have some real explanations to give regarding our whereabouts.

One of the things that I learned from my experience at that particular company, that will always be part of me, are the stories on rainy days. These were the days when it rained and the guys would sit by the door and compete at telling lies about their lives and other peoples' lives. This was also a time when guys in my group wanted to dress sharp, with all the latest clothes and some of the loudest colors. It wasn't unusual for us to be dressed in one loud color, such as lime, green, from head to toe.

When I was drafted into the Army, in December of 1969, I still couldn't shake off the style of dress, so I smuggled some of the clothing into my basic-training duffel bag, the ones that could be hidden under the uniform. I spent two years in the Army and most of the time in Germany. By the time I had been in Germany a few months all the loud clothing and fly attitude ended. While in Germany I learned to look at myself and my country with a more critical eye. I also realized that so much I did in the sixties was not real. In fact, I called it my dead decade or the dark period of my life. Germany was perhaps the greatest eye-opening experience for me ever; it prepared me for living in Fargo, ND.

Fargo was a new experience for me, I did not intend to stay here for so many years. My plan was to complete my education and return to

Germany where I had been established as a quality control tech in the printing ink industry from September 1972 until April of 1978. I thought that this was the career for me, and that I would always remain in that field. It allowed me to use my work to reinforce my avocation. Since my early school years art was a favorite subject for me and I explored every aspect of it that I could, particularly during the years that I worked for the German company.

Playing with endless colors was an enhancement to my creating works of art. I'll always have art to rely on throughout my life and I expect it to be my last career. My primary style of artwork is the urban/social landscape; I like to depict man and his environment. Of course I always go back to roots in South Carolina for inspiration for whatever I am involved in. Remembering my roots has always been important to the black community so it's only fitting that I do it often. However, I still marvel at miracle of my making it this far in my life and career. I could have been a victim of drowning in slingshot pond, railroad accident, or a lynching. I guess God has other plans for me.

Fargo has been good for me; in fact I've lived here longer than I've lived in any place, so in effect, it is home if the number of years has meaning. I came here to complete my education, after stopping-out of school for nearly fifteen years. I was a 34-year-old student/athlete at North Dakota State University when I started my college career again. The journey was tough, however it's been worth it, and I met with some success along the way. I've completed both undergraduate and graduate programs at NDSU, and I worked for the University for ten years. For the past ten years I've worked as an agent with State Farm insurance company, where I intend to work until retirement. My journey continues and I shall remain focused on developing my story.